FORBIDDEN PLACES
STRANGE FACES

Gavin Moles

authorHOUSE®

AuthorHouse™ UK Ltd.
1663 Liberty Drive
Bloomington, IN 47403 USA
www.authorhouse.co.uk
Phone: 0800.197.4150

A CIP catalogue record for this title is available from the British Library.

Published by AuthorHouse 05/12/2014

ISBN: 978-1-4969-7987-2 (sc)
ISBN: 978-1-4969-7988-9 (e)

Thank you to all my friends and family who have listened relentlessly to my ranting and raving over the past years; who have always encouraged me to pursue my dreams which has kept my imagination alive, helped me to confront my fears and dared to chase my dreams, finally telling me:

"For heaven's sake write a bloody book"

Therefore I would like to use this opportunity to thank all the individuals I have met along this great adventure of life who have contributed so much and enriched my life, experiencing so much compassion, kindness, and having shared such memorable time together. I will be forever humbled by such memories, and only hope to inspire others to dare to dream, and to explore all possibilities. Life is an adventure, a . . . . DISC OVER Y

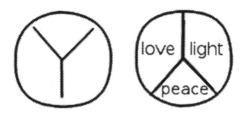

"Life is like riding a bicycle; you have to keep your balance so as not to fall off."

Albert Einstein.

"He who sees just a grain of sand in his hand only sees himself. He who sees the infinite in all things sees God"

William Blake

When a teacher asked John Lennon what he wanted to be when he grew up, he replied: "I want to be happy"

The teacher replied angrily "I don't think you understood the question"

He replied "I don't think you understood the answer"

Be Happy

Preface

Early days of adventure

Maybe the Jolly Welder had come into our lives for a reason, as part of a riddle that seemed to be unfolding before me, whereby I would discover an answer to a question which would lead me on to discover two more questions, exponentially accelerating towards a nervous breakdown or complete madness sugar coated with a hint of mysticism, trying to kill two birds with one stone and dancing on the yellow brick road to la la land to end up down that rabbit hole drinking tea with some unhinged hatter. These early days were often strange, uncertain but which made it all the more magical and full of daily surprises.

I had just left my job as a mechanic due to reasons that will become clear very soon which made me look for a change of direction that had me enrolling on a college course to pursue a more romantic and artistic career in media production.

Having a passion for art and being creative as much as possible was always a distraction for me as I became easily bored with the day to day dull routine, even with a huge imagination I failed to see how I could survive it, work, relationships, money, house, old age, pension boredom, regret, death. I was often caught day dreaming a solution to it all, and have always been ready for flights of fancy, any excuse to do something different, so when my Father telephoned to tell me he had seen a canal boat with a for sale sign on it, that looked like it was moored up at the bottom of a farmer's field, covered in crap, almost floating! on a very unpopular stretch of canal and was looking a bit neglected, therefore he thought it could be selling cheap and maybe I would be interested to take it on. After receiving his phone call and listening to his description, for some reason at that moment I knew this was it, inspiration . . . . adventure!

The more I thought about it all the more it took shape in my mind and the clouds of uncertainty suddenly parted. A bright light now shone from the heavens, which now illuminated the way ahead, because at this time I was standing at that crossroads of life wondering which way to turn, ahead of me now was a big arrow pointing towards the future, although in reality the letters where kind of unfashionable bright neon, blinking like a cheap hotel sign, but that did not matter I was inspired and nothing could go wrong.

"That is it! . . . . That is what we should do" I prophesied to my family, raving like a mad monk,

"Lets buy a boat, we can live on it, be pirates, river rats, whatever you want to call us, houses are boring, static and too expensive, we can do it another way" I fantasised.

Then in an instant, my mind tumbled through an infinite romantic boat scenarios . . . . and I was gone.

The boat seemed to me to be another element to the riddle, art, creativity and maybe a romantic way to escape the rat race a little, or just a crazy combined solution to fill the void of a boring college design brief that I was stuck with at this time which I had now thought to make a documentary about the journey from the Midlands from where it was moored, up to Harrogate north Yorkshire to where we were living, which is pretty much as far north as you can get by canal boat so no one really ever wants to go there, its a dead end!

There were a lot of ifs and buts at this time and more importantly very little money, but thinking as Moses turned out not to be so mad in the end with his interest towards boats I took it on, along with the support of my girlfriend at that time, our daughter and my first ever small loan from the bank.

On the first viewing of the 'Jolly Welder' it turned out to be an unfashionably home made affair, made by some enthusiastic DIY welder, that was obviously hiding behind a jolly name plate, of which I instantly took a shine to, because at this time I was still young, enthusiastic and my last job I had been working as a mechanic, whereby sometimes I found myself creating new bits of bodywork for old cars, cutting and welding pieces of steel together and I thought I was often jolly about it all, even on those cruel wintry days in the Yorkshire northern hemisphere, with numb, bruised knuckles, spannering away underneath an endless supply of snow covered customer cars, which melted, then dripped deliberately down the neck of my overalls, occasionally one would test my spirit even further by coughing up a belly full of spent diesel oil, or gearbox oil, which was terrible as the smell was so particular, and the taste, if you were unlucky enough at the time to have your mouth open, you could never quite get rid of the smell out of your nostrils, or the taste that clung to the back of your throat for the rest of the day. A few years in this trade and EP 80 gear oil for a vintage that was best forgotten.

Thinking about the name of the boat I felt a sort of destiny about it all and if any doubt creep in, all I had to do was re adjust those rose tinted glasses, until everything looked rosy and perfect. People often asked me: "Why are you so happy all the time, how do you do it?" Which often took me by surprise as I had not thought about such a question. I was just so naturally happy and enthusiastic with life, so I had not known what to answer them, looking back now it's easy to answer; I had a good imagination and a feeling that I could do anything if I put my mind to it, more importantly I could feel the universe conspiring with me, it was as excited as I was and therefore very happy to be conspiring with my thoughts, that whatever I thought about, the necessary particles of the universe suddenly manifested themselves somewhere just outside of my visual world, being born in the infinite quantum field of potential, which would then start to gravitated towards me and solidify into actual 'things'.

'The imagination has no boundaries' Einstein.

I never imagined I would ever fail at anything, or be disappointed; the only thing that ever really stops us from achieving things in this life is fear, often we fail before we have even tried.

Being a mechanic satisfied me for some time, satisfied my imagination and sense of curiosity to how things worked, so I enjoyed taking things apart, it was an adventure and a journey in itself if you like often into unknown territory, from which you returned with new experiences and knowledge. Fixing things, came hand in hand I suppose, with those rose coloured glasses combined with imagination and fuelled with a burning sense of adventure. Often my imagination would run away with itself and I would be lost in thought, day dreaming about infinite possibilities. I remember my school reports always making the same comments:

"Could try harder, too much time spent looking out the window and dreaming."

With the advances of quantum physics theory these days science seems to be observing exactly just that, that the mind effects matter, maybe creates it even, maybe if they did not look for certain particles, they would not exist, maybe all this is just my day dream, and we are all dreaming each other! Its not impossible.

Being a mechanic had its various problems and there were often times where I needed to relieve the tedium of it all, therefore for my amusement and sanity preservation I developed a catalogue of various vehicles in my mind, makes and models which I enjoyed personifying, giving them various characters and their associated attitudes, a bit like pets and their owners you got a sense of who would own a such and such.

Some were like well bred women that were well out of your league, the BMW's, Mercedes (blond haired with long painted finger nails, Daddy owns a Porsche, these were the type of high class rollers that you dreamed about and once in a while on a few rare occasions, you even got to fiddle with them. Whilst others just had attitude, they were the dregs of society and they did not want to be fixed in any way at all, had too long a life, too many miles on the clock and seen a lot of shit, their names were the abused Citroen's, Skoda's the formidable, and my own personal enemy, the hateful . . . . Fiat 126 . . . . these in my opinion were life's outcasts.

Fiat 126 . . . . my God!
What a vicious car that was, the only one
that very nearly sent me over the edge.

Normally I was a calm, happy, well spirited type, nothing could phase me . . . but this one occasion, which threatened to compromise my `Jolly Welder` attitude . . . . I came very close. This infamous, dreaded . . . . Fiat 126 . . . . No matter what frame of mind you approached them in, it always ended in tears, bruised knuckles, multiple lacerations and a new word that you had to invent, just so that you could insult it to the core of its design, but did it care? No!

"Naaaaaaaaa . . . . feck off." It rasped at me . . . . as I tried to approach it with a clear and calm professional attitude. "Cough, splutter . . . . keep yer ands off me ya Baaaaaaasssstad." It rasped at me again.

If Fiat 126's were a person it would be a small, fat, red faced Scottish tramp, high on special brew and stinking of piss, but that would be a big insult to tramps and not enough insult to Fiat 126's.

This was one of those special days that quickly became like a scene from Faulty Towers . . . . I was standing there, shaking with blind fury, poised behind its rear end, just out of its line of sight so that I could get the first blow in.

"You F . . . . G baaastard . . . . That's it . . . . I warned you."

My knuckles were already bruised, bleeding, my overalls had been viciously torn from deliberately sharpened body panels, it had swallowed one of my Snap On sockets and branded my arm for life with its hot exhaust whilst trying to retrieve it from the depths of impossible body work, designed to be just perfectly out of reach, exactly where the engine had been producing and leaking carcinogenic sludge, and just small enough with what felt like strategically positioned fish hooks, so as to lacerate your flesh when retracting your arm after touching the hot exhaust, after a few attempts of socket discovery and extraction, resulting in a few deep lacerations to the forearm whereby the carcinogenic sludge easily seeped in and absorbed into the epidermis, then quarterized and sealed in with a few exhaust burns. These cars were designed on a combination of days alternating between Fridays and Mondays; Friday being where everyone is pissed off and wanting to go home to the pub, therefore cutting corners, making mistakes and rushing through design deadlines, and Monday 'hangover' mornings, where no one can be arsed to produce anything sensible, and come up with design flaws deliberately just to piss someone else off so that they know how crap they are feeling.

I was seconds away from committing Fiat genocide. I stood there paralysed with rage, foaming at the mouth, and wielding my biggest hammer that I could put my hands on . . . . when suddenly had a flash, a premonition. I saw my future . . . . I was just seconds away from losing my job. I saw broken glass splintering all over the place, dented body panels, frantic slashing and bashing, oil and antifreeze draining away down the nearest manhole, to finally witness it's last pathetic groan, a defiant clunk, cough, and then a cloud of smoke rising up like a raised middle finger of final insult from its underpowered engine . . . . and then . . . . nothing, silence. It was dead. I was at peace!

A certain stillness came over me, as responsibilities were suddenly overruled by complete need to act. I cared not at all about losing my job against the satisfaction of beating this pile of crap to a much over due scrap yard burial. On a deeper level I think it was just a complete sense of defeat that came over me, failure, then anger, then an acceptance, a recognition of imperfection that not everything could be fixed in this world and that there are places for imperfections and this was one of those such cases, the phrase came to mind . . . .

"No matter how hard you try you just cannot polish a lump of shit."

With that new revelation I knew I had to get out of this line of work. I dreamt to be doing something more creative, beautiful and romantic, so I decided to go back to college and develop my artistic nature and express myself a little less aggressively with a paintbrush.

I was still young and unhindered by the onslaught of life, its baggage had not built up sufficiently yet to cloud the mind and judgement and had not developed too many fears, so I guess I was commonly known as not having any common sense and being irresponsible.

I was still wearing those rose tinted glasses, and therefore I did not see all the mould, condensation, rotting wood, and ignored the dank smell of unfashionable curtains and paisley patterns that would have caused even the strongest of minds to flash back to bad acid trips, whether you had ever tried any or not, I must say it was offensive in retrospect, but my vision were impervious to negativity and was brighter than ever before.

The owner was a round jolly character who had a slightly defeated, too many miles on the clock, or worked on too many Fiat 126s air about him and seemed obviously embarrassed by the condition the boat was in, constantly making excuses and apologies about it all; it was a funny situation, the worst salesman meets the perfect buyer, because I could not be disheartened by his apologies, my mind kept repeating it's mantra, a sentence to me that was sufficient to carry out the entire pirate adventure.

"it floats . . . . it's great, it's perfect, it just needs a little modernising . . . . I will buy it."

I repeated this to the owner; then again, and finally after the third time, he stopped apologising about the boat and realised I was serious, it was like lifting a curse for him, on that day the clouds parted for him and he almost seemed happy, or surprised more like!

I became the proud owner of The Jolly Welder, and a potential home owner for the first time. All that I needed to do now was to bring it up north, to Yorkshire and of course I had no idea how you would do that by the canal system from its present position in the Midlands up to, as close to Harrogate as possible. I promptly bought a canal guide book and quickly studied the route; there were not too many choices.

It was to be my first real adventure, a little journey of over 300 miles at walking pace. Only at this time the UK was experiencing severe drought, and many parts of the canals were restricted, which meant only allowing people passage who had moorings that they need to get to. We did not have any moorings as yet, or a canal licence, or a certificate of safety, or any idea of boats, locks or navigating a tidal stretch of river that was soon to be experiencing spring tides, and just for extra spookiness there was to be a solar eclipse exactly on the day we decided to travel on it, and set the scene for a perfect horror disaster movie.

That day came and we were waiting inside the lock that was a T junction which would open up and allow us access onto the river. Darkness had descended and turned daytime suddenly into night as the moon replaced the sun, flocks of birds took to the skies in confusion and panic, an eery drop of temperature taunted my soul whilst fumes from the prehistoric 2 cylinder Volvo Penta engine, filled the lock with a chocking smoke screen, my left hand was clammy with sweat as it gripped the throttle ready to go. Suddenly a loud Claxton sounded signalling that the lock gates were opening, slowly the huge black lock gates swung open and my eyes bulged in terror as I watched the river flowing past horribly fast which I estimated was twice the speed of my underpowered engine.

There was no going back now we were fully committed and firmly instructed by one of the British Waterways guys to . . . .

"Just floor it mate and go straight out, do not turn, do not pass go and collect your soiled trousers the next time around."

Assessing the whole situation very quickly I positioned my partner and our small daughter at the front of the boat, with life jackets on, instructing them as calm as I could whilst trying to hide the fact that I was crapping myself . . . .

"Be ready to jump off, I think we are having an adventure."

Well needless to say we and the boat did survive, not by skilful planning and experience of course but it certainly gave me a few stories to tell and maybe was the start to many more flights of fancy and adventures . . . . and of course it was.

It is my pleasure to be able to tell you about some of those adventures that have come and gone, some of which are still going on in my mind, my heart and hope by sharing these experiences with you now, that you too will dare to dream and imagine the impossible and know that we are all travelling together 'I and I' in this amazing, strange, beautiful, exciting uni-verse where all is one, somewhere just around the next corner, or the next person you meet, answers to our questions lay tantalisingly just out of reach, with each new sunrise we have survived another day, and another day awaits to be discovered, our eyes wide open with curiosity and wonder, this mirror of life reflects back to us what we often cannot see ourself.

'Ourselves'

To me there seems to be no coincidences, and if you dare to dream it, believe that it is impossible to fail, then already particles of the universe start to weave their magic, which sooner or later gravitate towards your goal, its goal, our goal, so when you find yourself in one of those situations where you are wishing that you were somewhere else, know that you have created it and it often means that you are probably having an adventure. I was encouraged by family and friends 'you should write a book' they said, so with their support and encouragement and in the spirit of adventure and unity, I truly hope you enjoy this journey with me.

And Shiva danced the particles of the universe into being.

Forbidden Places Strange Faces

Chapter 1

I left France on the 19th November at around 19:19am, to board a flight bound for Bangkok and took my seat in row 19a. I noticed these things and started thinking about various synchronisities, giving into superstition a little bit and allowing my imagination to enjoy a sense of significance to it all, but what, why, when and how I still have not worked that out yet, but I still like to take notice of these little details in life as I am sure it comes up with these things just to test who is paying attention or not . . . .

"Aha, you noticed." It said.

I think life likes people with a sense of adventure, those that dream it, dare it, do it, then life comes out from hiding to meet us half way. Life raised an eyebrow as I raised my rucksack up onto my shoulders.

I am excited to be travelling again, feeling privileged to have these freedoms as I started to reflect upon certain memories, remembering seeing such hardships and restrictions in other places that lifestyle, culture, religion and economic resources inhibited such freedom that I was now using for pleasure, or personal growth as I preferred to see it this time, because a few years ago I thought I was having some personal difficulties, so some close friends of mine, probably fed up with my moaning and groaning, convinced me I should go to Sri Lanka with them as a sort of therapeutic distraction, and yes it did very quickly stop me from feeling sorry for myself, seeing people in rags dragging themselves around on deformed limbs, whilst some of us were in bars the night before, then nursing and complaining about bad heads in the mornings; I therefore quickly sobered up.

In those days I had been having what I thought to be some bad turn of events in life and was feeling a little lost, dazed and confused, which was probably due to some of the great French red wine that I had discovered, found comfort in and became very happy with that year; many a bottle sat listening to my stories of true happiness and despair without judging me, it was a perfect relationship for a while, because in a way they were like women: they had such lovely bodies, perfectly formed, smooth curves, dark complexion, long neck, and no head . . . . Hmmmm! I chuckled to myself with that image in my mind, visualising a relationship with no arguments and total satisfaction . . . . yes another great year, let's do it again tomorrow my dear, hic!

Well my imagination never did need much to set it off spinning down some rabbit hole to appear in another world drinking tea with the mad hatter himself, so that year was a bit of a blur really with chasing rabbits down holes and apart from a little work that I was fortunate to pick up, it all occupied me well enough until something came along to inspire me further . . . . travelling! Well those first few steps into a totally different part of the world, culture, strange sounds, sights, smells, and real banana trees instead of the plastic ones in the supermarket, real fruit and vegetables that did not taste like plastic ones in the supermarket! Certainly aroused some dormant enthusiasm cells and I am eternally grateful to these caring people for helping me take these first exciting new steps towards the sun and light again, but maybe the travelling has become just another vice to substitute the other ones, as I found myself on that insatiable path of wanting to see more, go further, go higher.

This time I wanted a bit more of an adventure. I had a few months free and was travelling alone so the picture was a blank canvas with a full palette of colours. I had worked and saved a little money but the budget was very limited with just a few hundred Euro's and a return ticket, big adventure for few bucks was going to be the theme which limited me to walking as much as possible, hitch hiking, wild camping and preparing my own food. I had this urge to go to Tibet starting from Thailand and that was basically . . . . it!

Let It Begin

Chapter 2

Here I am waiting for the train to depart, that bridges the gap to all the possibilities that I imagined may be ahead; new faces, different places, strange situations that no doubt I will get into. I paused a little remembering something.

"Hmmmm . . . . yes must not do that this time . . . . no definitely that will not happen . . . . avoid monkeys . . . . yes."

I shuddered on that thought thinking about the time I nearly lost a finger to one of these cute, vicious little things in Thailand last year, now I have a severed tendon that still needs sewing back together. I entertained myself with previous episodes for some time whilst waiting for something to happen, then slowly something happened and I came back to the present. Life goes by when we are busy making other plans.

I had been in Bangkok now for over a week getting visas and equipment together, now I was sitting here waiting for the night train to leave which would take me to Chiang Mai. I was looking forward to the rhythm of the train to send me off to a much needed sleep as I was dizzy and still delirious from a head full of sleepless nights, and a fever which was set on from a good coating of Bangkok's finest filth which had decided to take up long term residence inside my delicate alveoli. Big cities were never my thing, with that and spending too long in the south of France I think all that clean air had done me no good, it has made me weak, vulnerable and susceptible to filth and hard conditions. Hence the pollution quickly got the better of me, sore throats soon followed, then fever and hacking up big lumps of Bangkok for too many consecutive nights, and so I was feeling pretty drained towards the end, eventually I decided to give into medication. I heard you could get some pretty good medication that you could never get in the west without prescription, so I went to a pharmacy and asked for something that would help me sleep, nod nod wink wink.

"These velly good, take two you sleep no ploblem, sure." . . . . the shop keeper assured.

Eager to try this chemical relief, I hurried back to my room remembering their recommended dosage of 2 and so took 4 to be sure . . . . and oh yes Mr. Sleep quickly came and smothered me like a warm blanket of infinite depth. I went out like a light but to my frustration I woke up two hours later dripping with sweat, and somehow tied in a double reef tangle knot with a wet bed spread. Seems like the fever had fermented whilst I had been unconscious. I must have been sweating like crazy and spinning around my bed like some possessed horror movie extra. Sleep had side stepped me again for yet another night.

I blearily wandered about inside the train, found my place and promptly curled up into a fetal position desperately hoping the train would rock me to sleep. Soon enough the train started to move. I revelled in this feeling for a while, the anticipation, the movement, the destination, to be getting closer to somewhere, to something . . . . the uncertainty . . . . yeah . . . it's great, OK but now I really want to sleep, please . . . .

It is amazing how life comes up with certain situations, how creative it can be when you are vulnerable in some way, it sometimes takes on a kind of immature, provocative, spiteful attitude, and this time it seems I am to be the only one who has the dodgy light fitting directly above me which is buzzing and flashing in a perfect way that would cause the strongest mind to go into a seizure, with that and synchronized with the manic 3 year old opposite, who is really pissed off, complemented the orchestra of annoyance specially designed to irritate a sleep deprived individual with . . . .

"Hmmmm yes thank you life, I can see how funny it must be to you."

Finally I managed to sleep a little and woke at around 7.30am. The train was chugging along happily, completely un-phased by annoying light fittings and hyperactive children. The smog and clutter of buildings were no longer being replaced with thick, green jungle like foliage which were now casually blurring past the windows. Real banana leaves were waving at me playfully, and my excitement hormones instantly duplicated themselves in anticipation to breathe this heady tropical concoction, perfume for my soul at last.

The train arrived and I was excited to get going again towards the next destination and head towards the border of Laos. I quickly located and got onto the relevant bus and settled down. Hours passed uneventfully apart from when a Thai man sort of came staggering over after first looking around at the various empty seats and promptly slumped himself down next to me. He tried to introduce himself, or at least that's what I thought he was doing, but maybe he was just trying to balance, or to think, the clue came a few seconds later as he started waving his can of 'Chang beer' around a lot and dribbling. I was surprised to see that he was also carrying a small baby that also clung to him in the same way that he was clinging on to his beer can. The baby also introduced himself by wobbling and dribbling a lot, both were now dribbling very well, swaying, trying to focus on me, then in front, to the side, the floor, and then suddenly they both loomed towards me, maybe in a desperate attempt to try to bridge the gap between east and west, but in this case maybe there was not enough saliva to describe such a huge divide in cultures, but fair play to him, he tried which is more than what I tried to do, instead I judged him, tried to ignore him, and in the end was intimidated by him, but he used his best native slurring instead, and finally broke my concentration of denial. I had a relationship with a Thai woman for a few years so I had picked up a few words here and there, but my ability was still very basic at the best of times and I quickly realized was completely useless against Chang beer and so we continued the charade, he dribbled, his baby dribbled grappled and clawed all over both of us whilst he just smiled, drank, dribbled and occasionally spat out some words . . . .

"dee sanuk, koaw jai?"

Good fun, you understand?

Eeeeeek . . . . why me I think to myself, always I seem to attract the drunk and the dribbling and the strange thing was that no one else seemed to notice him, so I presumed it was just normal for them I supposed, after all what is normal? Only that which we are used to! Thai man drunk in charge of infant nothing special, it's just a test I remind myself, its just showing me things. OK I get the picture I thought to myself, but can we move on from this now. I tried not to judge too much and started to take interest in trying to humour the infant, feeling a bit sorry for him, it's not his fault not his choice, then shortly after that realization they got up and left at the next stop.

Search And Destroy

Chapter 3

I finished the last few spoonfuls of my 'Kow Tom' soup, which is a thin soup stock made with rice, minced pork, garlic, and chili which makes for a very warming and satisfying `pick me up` which my partner used to make for me when I had a cold or not feeling too good, it really did pick me up, and I started to drift off with memories of her swimming around in my mind, the good times, the bad times . . . errrrrrr . . . . yeah OK, move on.

I watched for an unknown length of time, hypnotized with the layers of early morning mist as it mysteriously animated itself, moving like some primordial spirit which was seeking, searching, sensing, it seamlessly shape shifted into various forms and now there were ghostly tendrils just above tickling the surface of the Mekong river, which was looking like a scene from 'apocalypse now' it was a river of deep thick orange yellow like soup where soon we were to be crossing, not by search and destroy tactics this time but by some little tourist ferry boats, with grinning toothless operators sat at the rear in what looked like long wooden canoes with over sized car engines that were powering a long drive shaft which had a propeller bolted on to the end of it, like some over engineered egg whisk that a petrol head would invent. With a twist of the wrist they sped quickly to the other side, and back again eager to ferry more waiting tourists.

I was regretting the early start now as I gazed upon the hoards of other people trying to pass through this tiny little outpost, and so I resigned myself to the fact that there would be lots of queuing, bits of paper, passports, confusion and money exchanging hands. I headed out into that jungle of formalities, with a 'grin and bare it' attitude taking pleasure and amusement with all these different people, characters, accents, styles, and of course toothless old men who were still grinning away. I think they had seen it all since the beginning of time and probably knew how it was all going to end, hence the infinite grin. Life is the ultimate comedy it seems, the true nature of which it is said by many 'enlightened beings' if you see it, when you see it, you will know you have because you cannot describe it, because it is so bizarre, so extraordinary, so unbelievable simple to the point of being insanely perfect, all you can do is laugh, in fact you will not be able to stop laughing. The infinite being, God, Buddha, Krishna and all the other plethora of personified deities, including and especially including ourselves . . . . do have a wicked sense of humour it seems.

His grin did seem to have a wicked knowingness about it all, and I almost wanted to sit down and grin alongside him for eternity, it looked good, peaceful and I don't think he had ever worked on Fiat 126s.

Finally the formalities were over with and I headed out with very little idea of where to go, so I thought to just follow the general direction of tourist Jeeps which in the end all seemed to be going towards Luangnamta I hopefully presumed. I decided to stop and ask a few local people not sure if they understood me or not, but they listened and with bemused smiling faces, they gestured the way and 'Sabadee' me on my way. I got my compass out fantasizing about a little short cut through the jungle and read east with a bit of north. I looked up at the general direction to approach a sea of green rolling hills, with a single tarmac highway cutting through it all, it felt good to be on foot, with my backpack again, my tent and everything I needed to be autonomous on the way the first few steps through Laos towards China.

I was hoping to have found the way out on some dusty old track, romantically hacking a trail through the jungle and quaint timeless villages, well maybe a few years ago it was like that but now it was a tarmac highway. Sporadic villages scattered along the way, rustic wooden structures built on high stilts buzzing with village life, from which shy looks and excited faces peer out from every house, fingers pointing and children giggle as I plod past them with my small guest house on my shoulders. I try to imagine what fascinates them, is it the way I look? The way I walk? My clothes? I wondered what I actually look like to them. I wished for a moment that I could see through their eyes and peer into their mind, maybe the experience of that would break the spell of self consciousness and embarrassment. In my mind I look at them no different to me except we are in different situations and opportunities of life, we are all basically the same. We are all travellers.

The day started to get very warm, heat was radiating off the surface of the black tarmac road and up ahead on the horizon was shimmering a silvery mirage, whilst under my feet the road was spotted with glistening patches of melting black tar. With over 170 km to the Chinese border, the romance of walking looked like it could wear off pretty soon, but I reminded myself I am on the way now, just relax, don't rush and enjoy the moment, with the feeling that it all has a bearing on the journey, so I started to relax into a steady pace and thought what it would be like camping in the jungle somewhere tonight, imagining and building up a suitable scene in my mind, under the stars to be re united at last with nature who I had developed a strong passion with these last few years whilst exploring France and the mountains of the Pyrenees, days, weeks months walking, sleeping under the stars had bought me back again to simplicity, nature, humility, and more importantly, peace.

Finally I ended the day having travelled about 65km, thanks to a couple of precarious motorbike rides which had me perched on the back with a heavy rucksack that wanted to go in the opposite direction every time he accelerated. My forearms ached afterwards but it was a good opportunity to speed up this part of the road, satisfied with the day and no need to push on I found a quiet place to set up camp for the night, where there was cool running water gently trickling down from a stream which I quickly took advantage of to wash the days dust and sweat away. Soon I was refreshed, clean and my little camp organized. I made a drink and sat smug within with my little encampment and found a place to sit under a small bamboo shelter that some of the local people must have built to protect them from the midday sun and settled down to watch the flamingo pink sky slowly turn into night. Gradually one by one the first few stars appeared. It was that magical hour of half light, mysterious, transitional and thought provoking. Was I observing it or was it observing me? I revelled in this sensation trying not to think about it all too much, listening to the new sounds, smells and sensations of my first night out in the jungle, allowing various thoughts and sensations to come and go unhindered as they flowed through various sensory circuits. After some time I started to feel the chill of the night, temperature inversion and the damp of the night suddenly descended like a blanket. I lit a fire to complete the ritual that I felt appeased some ancient instincts of warmth and security. I did feel warm and secure that night, wrapped in mother natures arms she gently cradled me into deep satisfying sleep.

I awoke in the morning, feeling refreshed and invigorated taking in a good lung full of clean air to savour the morning freshness, groaning, stretching and clicking various bits of me back into position. I felt good. The air was still cool and damp with the sweet smell of dew soaked grass permeating the air, the tent was completely soaked with the humidity, but very quickly with the rising sun its strength soon had tendrils of steam rising up and quickly drying everything a little before setting off.

It was an uneventful morning plodding along the same road, but just as the road was getting more hot, hilly and less and less interesting to be walking on, I started thinking how nice it would be to speed up this part of the journey, almost immediately a pick up truck stopped just ahead of me with a cargo of Chinese looking people loaded with bags of rice, potatoes, chickens, clothes which were all crammed together like a human jumble sale, very kindly but with a strange insistence, they seemed to be offering me a lift, frantically gesturing me to get in the back. They did not say anything or even ask if I wanted to, motioning me to just climb on the back, no need to try to communicate, they knew I wanted to go this way, everyone wanted to go this way I suppose. I decided to accept as there will plenty of other opportunities for walking later on and just go with the flow. I clambered into the back and apologetically wedged myself in within the jumble of bodies, bags, toothless smiles and settled into what became a very bumpy, dusty ride, but I was quickly appreciative and grateful as the road became more and more elevated with miles and miles of tarmac twisting through the jungle, funny how things seem to happen just at the right time and it certainly would not be the last.

Finally after a few hours of being bashed about, stiff and slightly bruised with intimate relations established with many varieties of vegetables we arrived in Lluangnamta, which was the border town to China. The choice was fortunately quite simply to pick a direction up or down a long road with non significant buildings strewn either side, shacks and stalls. I chose to go what I thought was up the street and stopped at the nearest place that served food so that I could sit down, get my bearings and wash myself down a bit. After enjoying a good feed I was feeling more relaxed and I decided not to push on any further deciding to look around the local villages exploring and taking in the atmosphere, it was a very peaceful and simple place, like being back in medieval times, weaving looms, basic tools hanging up, things drying out in the sun, goats, dogs, cats, chickens you name it was running around all over the place, where one family started and the other one ended was a mystery so that I think even they just mingled, shared and got on with it all. I felt like I was in a film set, it was unreal. I drifted past it all not aware of my feet, what direction I was going as though I was on a timeless escalator ride, a voyeur of which I felt very out of place in a strange alien landscape, all eyes watched me with curiosity and amusement giggling and smiling..

I struggled to find anywhere discreet to put up my tent and decided hat if I could not be discrete, then to do the opposite and found a place between two houses on some waste ground. I emerged from my tent in the morning, stretching and clicking my bones back into their relevant sockets, enjoying the sun rays on my skin to notice a small local audience gathering, eyes peering through windows and standing on porches waiting for the show to start, not shy to stare at us like we are with each other, so I carried on with my mornings performance for them of cleaning, feeding then packing everything away. Finally I smile, wave and 'Sabaidee' to them, shyly they wave and smile back and I go on my way.

Pink Fluffy Nightmares
Of The Soul

Chapter 4

Today I needed to get to the Chinese border and being a person who does not plan things too much with no guide books or information, `just winging it` as usual, I did my usual bit of walking aimlessly around, following conflicting directions from locals as to where a bus station might be which wasted a few hours until I became aware and to accept that there did not seem to be one, but I did find everything else that I absolutely did not need. Eventually I found a place where a few private vans were waiting, offering transportation services and found one of them that was to go out to the border. I handed over some money for a seat in one of them and without any instruction as to what time or what day even it might happen, I promptly waited around for something to happen. Whilst waiting for something to happen I notice a young Chinese woman who for some reason caught my eye . . . . no, nothing like that I was not particularly attracted to her; just something about her that I found interesting that I could not pin point, but it grabbed my attention and kept me watching; like a movie that you cannot decided if it is good or bad but you are compelled to keep watching out of curiosity to see what the end will be like. I did have an uncontrollable curiosity that kept me watching, but I did not get to see the end of this movie past, present or future and I saw no conclusion to my interest here and now. I forced myself to change the channel and watch something else instead: like crisp packets blowing in the wind; a dog pissing up the tyre of a car; a man kicking the dog . . . . I take a glance at my watch again, it was just a few minutes advanced from the last time I looked, and so I decided to carry on with the Chinese girl watching.

Until it was her who finally broke the ice. I was sitting inside the small shuttle van quietly deep inside a special compartment of my mind, until her curiosity compelled her to make a move and leant over my shoulder to look at the photos I was flicking through on my camera, a sharp playful female voice said something which funnelled down my ear and broke through into my inner space. female! . . . . I promptly jumped, not expecting something or anything to invade me from behind like that and that's how we met, so we chatted and quickly caught up on who what where and why, what it was all about and where we were going, sharing stories and information, it was an instantly open and comfortable encounter. She told me that she was a writer, of love stories apparently and she had been travelling around Laos and was now returning back to China with no major plan for a month or so and I learnt that we seem to be travelling pretty much in the same direction, sounding like a good love story in the making I entertained to myself, but I was happy with the encounter, the company the opportunity to share stories and again it was good timing as not having been to China before I thought it could be nice to have some guidance for a few days until I get the feel of the place, and just as I had thought these things she appeared . . . . plooof . . . . in the form of Watsumei . . . . a bubbly, crazy, chatty, Chinese travelling buddy, she was a real help with the language barrier for sure and a wealth of local information. Sometimes I feel it's like something decides for me at times . . . . OK now you need a translator and guide for this bit, and it manifests one or creates a situation for me.

We spent a few days travelling together, making our way northwards up through the beautiful province of Yunnan and all was very interesting until one day everything changed and became . . . . pink! Discovering that two is company three is a definitely a crowd! That particular day Watsumei came back from a shopping spree, grinning wildly about her new bright pink baby chicken!

"only one dorrar, velly cheap" she grinned.

Hmmmmm OK ten out of ten for cuteness and weirdness but this thing soon became a cute, pink nightmare, it just would not stop chirping, just incredible how such a small thing could produce such torture, such ear piercing, relentless noise.

We decided to go window shopping to pass some time whilst we waited for our next bus . . . . it came with us, chirping none stop . . . . chirp, chirp, chirp, chirp . . . . we sat and tried to relax and enjoy the scenery . . . . it came with us and continued to . . . . chirp, chirp, chirp, chirp . . . . We ate lunch . . . . it came with us . . . . chirp, chirp, chirp, chirp . . . . I put it in my hat, still it kept chirping and chirping and chirping. People were looking at the hat, looking at us, chirp, chirp, chirp, chirp . . . . I shrugged. I tried to feed it, water it, stroke it, talk to it, begged it, and even prayed to it to . . . .

"Please for the love of God . . . . stop chirping will you, damn it"

I put it into my bag and closed the top, chirp, chirp, chirp . . . . hang on why am I getting all the sibling grief here I thought to myself? OK normally when I meet a girl I get to carry bags and maybe have to put up with a bit of boring shopping, shoes, handbags, but now its chicken rearing . . . . and bloody bright, girly pink one at that too, how do they do that anyway?

As time passed the chirping continued relentlessly, it became obvious to me that we had no life any more, we did not talk to each other, could not remember the last time we smiled or looked at each other without hoping the other would 'deal with it' I was distraught. I did not know what to do this thing was driving me, us nuts, we were not smiling any more.

Later I nervously decided to break the news to her as I know through previous experiences how some Asian women can get very sensitive and emotional when confronted, and I was still healing from some of those confrontations that were still finding it hard to flow under that bridge of time . . . . yes baggage!

"Watsumei . . . . you . . . . you know, you can't keep it, you know, it's lovely and pink and cute and fluffy and all that, and it was such a great idea of yours to buy it, take care of it, cuddly it (to death hopefully . . . . I just thought that I did not dare to say it!) but it will drive us . . . no it will drive me insane"

Her deep dark eyes looked at mine through ever narrowing slits knowingly, an Asian seriousness and silence ensued, old memories of such confrontations bubbled up and formed small beads of fear and anxiety, whereby I was not sure if she wanted to cry or to stick the fork in my head that she was nervously fiddling with, either way something had to be said, and inside my soul cringed waiting for the inevitable.

That evening back at the guest house the chicken drama continued, this little cute pink pet had been chirping itself into a small fluffy frenzy, the pitch and repetition increased so much until finally the last tolerance cell in my mind could not take it any more and immediately out of sheer desperation it invented a pair of strong hands so that it could commit suicide and promptly throttled itself, as it ceased to be something else decided to act.

"Jesus we have to do something with this thing"

I blurted out then quickly scooped it up in my hands and stormed out of our room, instinctively I knocked on the door of the adjacent room where I found myself introducing ourselves to two European girls . . . .

"Oooooh . . . . Hi girls. Look what I have, it's great isn't it, it's amazing, it's the ideal travelling accessory . . . . just look how cute and pink it is . . . . look, sorry but you know we are in a bit of a hurry and need someone we can trust to take care of this special pink travelling accessory . . . . here I am giving it to you, it will bring you luck, it's yours take it . . . . thank you, goodnight"

. . . . Woooosh . . . . slam . . . . I was out of there hoping it would appeal to some fluffy, pink compartment of their brains . . . . but oh no, two minutes later, knock knock! . . . . no way they returned it.

"Its damn rude to return a gift you know!!!"

Various cells in my mind started to get very nervous indeed, chirp, chirp, chirp, chirp . . . . arrrrgh! This is like some twisted Tweety Pie Halloween night special, it was back . . . . more pissed off than ever, this thing is going to send me over the edge. I thought about it for a moment, a flash of inspiration I felt a brilliant idea was hatching, but then I realised I had no more sleeping pills left, damn it! Finally Watsumei took on her part of the parental role and decided to take it to the guest house owner as she noticed they had kids, so either it will get hugged to death or annoy them so much it will end up in some Chinese won ton soup, morality was not the option any more but at least we both slept well that night although I had trouble with the little round faces I kept seeing of Chinese kids eating won ton soup and spitting out pink feathers on to the floor.

Crazy Chinese! I was a little dazed but amused and tickled pink with feathers of the mind as I drifted in and out of sleep and floated upon impossible, impassable roads to Lhasa. Thoughts were swimming around inside my head like a full load in a washing machine, there was too much soap and too many bubbles, and somewhere within were a whirlpool of images, conversations and various advice from different people who I had met and asked about how to get into Tibet. One thing kept repeating and going through my mind that everyone kept telling me:

"It is forbidden and impossible for a foreigner to travel into Tibet alone"

I stretched out on my bed and let my imagination decide what was impossible or not and meditated upon the journey ahead. It was now December and very cold at night reaching minus double figures and I thought about what to do when I reached the last town of Dequin, as there would still be over a thousand kilo-meters of uncertainty before reaching Lhasa; then from there I had the idea of continuing on into Nepal. There were a few problems though: I had no map; no permit; no idea of weather conditions and basically no idea. The washing machine kept spinning and spinning until I came up with a certain philosophy that eased my mind which was this: If I stop thinking and stop trying plan then what could possibly go wrong . . . . nothing!

Tomorrow we arranged to go to Kunming as it was still on the way for me and an opportunity for me to meet up with some of Watsumei's friends, who she was looking forward to catch up with again after returning from her little trip to Laos. I started wondering though if this would be a wise move and imagined the worst case scenario of being seriously outnumbered and the risk of drowning in a sea of 1 dollar multicoloured frantic chirping avian fledglings.

I had a chilling feeling that from now on the way ahead is going to get colder, and crazier maybe but I got to go with this crazy Chinese roller coaster ride. After all this is what it was all about, the uncertainty, the lessons, the challenges, the adventure, and the memories.

We booked some tickets to Dali, which was a 17 hour bus ride from here to the higher altitudes of the north west, then after there I wanted to get to the legendary 'Shangri-La' and check out the possibilities of getting a bus ride to Lhasa, but the more people I started asking about this possibility the more they are all shaking their heads and telling me things that I don't want to hear.

"For a foreigner travelling alone, no way it's impossible, it's forbidden"

The only way to travel through Tibet is to sign up for a tour, join a group and pay silly money, no way not for me to organized, too restrictive and more importantly too expensive. I decided to go with one bit of advice a friend gave me which was to just jump onto a bus and play dumb if anyone asks you any questions . . . . yeah that's more like my style, I thought . . . . I'll just wing it. Just have to get as far as I can and see how the land lies when I get there, or I'll walk . . . . !

Take Me To Shangrila
la la la laaaaaa...

Chapter 5

I stayed two nights in Dali, enjoying the atmosphere of Chinese culture which was a total immersion of the senses for me and could not help thinking how completely Chinese it all was, I know that sounds strange but it was like being on a movie set, and so visually stimulating, the architecture, the people and all the stereotypes were there, the Fu man Chu moustaches, the strange smells and sights, cats and dogs on the street and on your dinner plate. I finally left there with a new inventory of memories, strange relations and even stranger nights in dizzy Chinese bars.

It seemed a very easy place here and definitely too easy to get caught up into the night life, a carnival atmosphere of Chinese lanterns, bright lights rich, vibrant, fun atmosphere of culture. It was very stimulating and I found everyone to be so laid back, relaxed, happy, friendly, smiling, smiling, smiling and . . . . ooooh . . . . stoned! . . . . all the time day and night spending a bit of time amongst these people it was hard not to appear or feel a little uptight compared to some of these spaced out star children 1960s flashbacks.

I have to admit I had my one night of weakness and allowed myself that privilege. That particular night I was feeling a little lonely after being blown out by Watsumei for reasons I never really got to the bottom of, consoling myself to the fact that it was just another movie that I did not get to see the end of. I also presumed it to be some sort of post pink chicken depression, so I left her that night with her friends and I came across a bar where I had been in the previous night and had met the owner, who was another, bubbly, chatty, smiley, crazy Chinese woman of colourful character, but more importantly she had no pink chickens!

I walked into the bar, it was pretty quiet that night and I saw the owner sitting down at a table by herself. I casually sat down opposite, smiled and said hello, she looked up recognized me and instantly went into over animation mode, one of these people who just speak exactly what is happening in their mind without any filtering taking place. I liked that and so consequentially we chatted, joked, laughed, smoked a bit of this and drank a bit of that enjoying the spontaneity, her mother came over who talked at me in Chinese, I shrugged back and smiled which must have worked because she then went off and cooked us all food. We ate, talked, laughed then out came the red wine . . . oh oh I thought to myself . . . . that old red devil, my brain tried to warn me but by this time my lower brain was not listening, I was already gone and that lower brain was too caught up with the atmosphere, the spliff, the red wine and feeling fully immersed in another type of Chinese culture and fantasizing about a little Chinese romance . . . . a little more wine maybe? another spliff? no, no, no . . . . I shouldn't . . . . my mind divided and now I have Satan on one shoulder and my guardian angel on the other . . . .

"have a joint, drink some wine, its just a bit of fun, go on what's the harm" one of them barked.

"No no no don't do it you will regret it tomorrow, you will end up losing control because you will get totally drunk and wake up the next day with a bad head and most of my

money missing along with important parts of your memory"
the other interrupted.

I stopped and thought for a least a second about it
all . . . . hmmmmm morality, responsibility . . . . arrrrgh! it
was too difficult to think about it all now, so gave in and I
let my lower brain take me to Shangri-La . . . . take me to
Shangri-La la la laal alaaal alalaaa.

Another bottle of wine later, another spliff . . . the
guardian angel was now a distant echo overpowered by
the heady atmosphere, we were intoxicated caught in this
moment of uncontrollable laughing, dancing, joking . . . .
grinningly wildly, that red faced devil was now taking a full
front seat, fuel injected highway ride to hell . . . .

"Well hell seems to be alright after all" I think to myself,
at least it is warm, the wine is good, this spliff is making
me smile like a Cheshire cat and this Asian demoness looks
harmless enough, she's purring like a kitten, twisting,
dancing writhing, hmmmmm! we just having fun, she's
cute, funny, happy, good body and . . . . hmmmmmmm its
been a while, yes very good body language going on, or is it
just the red wine in my head? . . . . I can't tell any more . . . .
"hey I got to stop talking to myself now she might notice"

We were dancing now flowing along with the music
in a totally empty bar deep inside China just the two of
us, the emptiness was strange it was like some private
fantasy that a dream had suddenly and three dimensionally
materialized. Maybe I am on the holl-odeck of the star ship
enterprise I surmised, yes that's it at some point during the
evening Dr.Spock must have mind melded me and ran a
simulation through my mind, I will wake up soon grinning
and dribbling on the holl-odeck with a fleet of Klingon
battle cruisers just about to attack. I paused for a moment
and thought my senses almost came back for an instance,

then as I watched her dancing, babbling away to herself and realized I was not the one for concern, that she is completely hat stand crazy, Lucy in the sky gone with diamonds . . . . and she's gone, gone, gone . . . . I take a mental photograph and save it for later, just too weird at the moment to think about it all, then I select some more songs on a nuke box and turn the music up full, we both explore these vibrations our bodies dancing, testing each others space, she's like some feline shadow shifting from woman to cat, twisting purrring, teasing, damn it! she knew what she was doing. Too much power.

"OK" she announces and grabs my arm with a sharp tug in the direction of the door

"we go party now, you will be my party buddy for tonight"

Obediently I followed her out; well not exactly followed but kind of staggered out, as though under some sort of spell, something like what a very heavy moth would try to do as it desperately tried to reach some far away impossible light. We went out into the street and very soon entered into another bar but by now the fresh air and impossible distance had really got the better of me. The world was spinning and I was feeling a little out of my comfort zone from one extreme to the other, finally to enter a smoky haze of local people. I walked around a little dazed amongst the purple haze and slanted eyes, a crazy carnival of confusion whereby I suddenly found myself wanting to be somewhere else; I tried to use my own words of encouragement and attempted to remind myself that I was probably having an adventure.

Then maybe an internal warning bell or some other unfair instinct decided it was time I should go. I quickly came around to my senses that were in full warning . . . . alarm . . . . alarm . . . . alarm . . . . something was telling me to abort, to get out. Upon seeing the exit sign flashing in the distance I discretely left, along with my remaining brain cells where she remained as a memory of laughing and dancing with someone I hardly new but the warmth of that encounter will remain with me forever, and of course I felt good that I had survived another day.

The following day did arrive and as a reward for my better judgement, my head was an acceptable mess and was definitely time to move on. I was eager to put things behind me and to make progress northwards to the next village of Lijiang.

Within the busy town of Lijiang lies the old part from which it had originally expanded, it consisted of a maze of ancient buildings, a labyrinth of alleyways and many souvenir shops, restaurants and rustic fairy tale guest houses, despite the carnival atmosphere tat was perfectly designed towards extracting as much as possible from passing tourists, it did not distract in any way from its charm, because it was just complete eye candy for the eyes and even more unbelievable at night, a real Chinese fairy land, illuminated streams alive with exotic fish adding to the festival of colours, Chinese lanterns and attractive displays of fresh food, a real walk through fairy tale town, and yes lots of those tempting Chinese bars.

I arrived within the old city and became quickly hypnotized with its charm and its labyrinth of alleyways that was leading me this way and that, teasing my curiosity that I kept wanting to see what just around the next inviting archway, my eyes were struggling to take it all in, somewhere in the background of my mind a faint audience was cheering, oooooooing and aaahhhhing, but before I got too involved in it all I reminded myself to find a guest house first and then come back out to explore. Upon finding the first guest house I came across I did not waste too much time and went through all the formalities as quickly as possible, filling in registers, passports, room key, money . . . . great, off I went. I have this terrible curiosity and kind of greediness that I want and need to see absolutely everything and would feel very annoyed with myself if at a later point if I realized I had missed something really amazing whilst I was there. Therefore I was determined to absolutely explore it all.

Hours passed like a dream time and I was almost satisfied that I had successfully seen all that there was to see within this part which I realized was just a fraction of what were there. It was just starting to get dark so I thought I had better get back to my room and change into something warmer for the evening, then a sudden thought came into my mind when one and one suddenly made two and parts of my mind was starting to be responsible again. In my haste to get out and explore I did not take any mental note as to where my guest house was, did not take a card, could not remember the name of the place, had no money with me, was getting quite hungry, cold and tired at this point so my mind was not as sharp as it normally wasn't and struggled to come up with a brilliant solution.

"you bloody idiot" I told myself, this curiosity of mine has got me into another fine mess. Needles to say it took hours to eventually retrace my steps, stopping in various places and trying to remember if I recognized a particular Chinese lantern, or alleyway, or building, that all looked very familiar, until eventually I blundered down what I thought was another blind alley only to find it was here all along.

The next morning I climbed up the nearest hill to get a better view of the surrounding area and maybe also hoping to reach a little bit closer to the heavens, then maybe God would take pity on me and do a bit of re-wiring whilst we were at it; I was still thinking about the hours of wandering around last evening and the stupidity of it all.

I was on top of a good sized hill and from here was an excellent 360 degree panorama view, a huge plateau and distant white capped mountains. I had heard about a place that was about 3 hours away from here called 'Tiger leaping Gorge' and decided it would be a good place to start walking. It was a deep valley where the Himalayan waters had cut through on its journey from the top of the world down to the southern regions. This was to be the first little walkabout a few days free from buses and busy towns and was said to be about a 2 to 3 day hike, then after I was hoping to find some trails that I could follow on foot to the legendary Shangri-La and then on to Dequin, which was the last town before Tibet. I was hoping to get as far north as possible and then try to buy a bus ticket to Lhasa, but it all sounded too easy and simple I wanted a bit of an adventure, a challenge. I am not the sort of person who likes to plan things out too much or research as it leads to disappointment when things don't go to plan or you read into things, information comes to you that might put you off from trying, so this time I managed to find a large scale map of Asia and decided to start here, go there, then here and hopefully end up there, packing my rucksack with enough things to be completely independent, tent, cooker, dried food, some mountain equipment, maps and a head full of adventure. What could possibly go wrong?

There are tribal people here in this region called the Naxi people who were once a nomadic race living a life very similar to the red Indians of America, and like them they regarded themselves as the great caretakers of the planet and in return for their respect and services, nature had shown them a wealth of natural knowledge which assisted them to live in complete harmony with their surroundings, only taking what they needed, always replacing and keeping the balance in order. They have their own special language similar to hieroglyphics, pictorial representations of ideas and concepts for the description of daily life, over the centuries it had become more refined and eventually evolved into the Chinese characters used today, it was very interesting to learn some of these characters and to understand their pictorial roots, the meanings were very beautiful and poetic descriptions. The Naxi only obtain daily necessities and try their best to keep the ecological balance, they consistently uphold a primitive Shangri-la-spirit (which means a harmony between human and nature) I like to know about these sort of people, some people think of them as uneducated, superstitious and even savages because of the strange way they live, their clothes or in some cases the lack of them, their superstitions that we do not identify with or understand, we are taught to fear things we do not understand, we live in a world of division and prejudice, and media propaganda. Yet a lot of our western medicines and advances in research come from these type of people who have lived very close to nature, studied her, observed her and finally she reveals her knowledge, these people and had to respect her to survive, knowing both species, all species need each other. A huge percentage of all our western medicines were synthesized from knowledge discovered from indigenous peoples, much of which comes from the Amazon and its millions of species of plants. I read an account written by an anthropologist who had been staying in a remote village in the Amazon documenting their way of life and was amazed with the knowledge that the Shamans had of everything even knew about human DNA and could describe its double helix, and had huge extensive knowledge of the plants, their chemical composition, preparations which could and did cure serious illnesses. How? after all these people were uneducated, uncivilized, how could they possibly have any knowledge or wisdom. After a long conversation one night this anthropologist kept asking about how they knew what they did, who taught them, where did this knowledge come from? a Shaman spoke to the anthropologist, he said "how many years have your people been educating themselves in your institutions, schools, colleges, universities?" the anthropologist thought about this and replied "well I suppose we have had these schools, colleges and universities for a few hundred years or so" and the shaman replied "well we study directly with nature, who is our teacher for everything in our University out there that is the jungle everyday for ten thousand years"

We have much to learn still about our world and the variety of things that inhabit it, things that I am sure we all used to know long ago but since have got lost along the road of progress, distracted by our over complicated, plastic fantastic, wasteful, successful lifestyles that only serves to keep us slaves as the things that we think we own become to own us in the end.

Quiatao And The
Tiger Leaping Gorge

Chapter 6

I missed the early bus but soon caught another one which took us directly out into the countryside, down long twisting roads passing by small villages and farms, eventually becoming more rugged and mountainous, until finally arriving in Quiatao at around 3pm. A disappointing place after passing by so many cute traditional Chinese scenery, we arrived at this rough uninspiring, grey, dirty, road side town. With obviously not much to see I quickly found and booked into a suitable room of equally uninspiring concrete grey, dirty, cold and broken appearance, but I was feeling much closer to where I wanted to be; I could feel adventure and nature whispering to me that was just a breath away. Already the scenery had elevated dramatically and either side were high mountains and jagged peaks of white surrounded us. I was eager for tomorrow, needing a change from all the distractions; too many bus rides , too many pink chickens, weird woman and not enough walking and exploring that I had dreamt I would be doing.

I tried to settle down in my luxurious room but a cool breeze kept blowing through the missing glass in the window. I could feel the evening chill rapidly descend as the warmth of the sun quickly disappeared behind dark jagged rock and the mountain shadows moodily enveloped the valley with an icy darkness. I shivered as the air started to cut through the thin layers that I was wearing so I put on another and I got out my camping stove to make a warm drink. Soon I had a steaming cup of tea and I snuggled deep into my sleeping bag then switched on the TV.

Wow it worked!

Surprised, I did expect nothing to happen thinking that it was there just to make the room look more furnished than it wasn't and that probably everything inside had been removed to repair someone's obsolete digital watch.

I systematically flicked through the many dancing, cute, fluffy, pink chicken adverts. 'God knows what that's all about I thought?' Then finally my mind settled and became engrossed as it came across the start to an old kung foo movie.

"Aaah this is great" I thought very fitting and atmospheric. I quickly became transfixed, overlooking all the bad lip sinc and acting, just instead admiring the choreography of it all, arms and legs flying around all over the place, truly incredibly when you think about it all, there must have been no special effects in those days just damned hard training, focus and dedication, a trait to which I had been noticing throughout China, and many other places that I had travelled through; these people seem to have a great level of dedication and skill, and can do anything they put their minds to. I remember looking at some silk tapestries a few days ago. I became amazed at what they were doing, the more I looked at what they were doing and how they were doing it the more I could appreciate such mind blowing attention to detail and patience. These incredible pictures were made by stitching what looked like practically microscopic fine strands of different coloured silk. Each strange was pre selected and graded before into various colours, shade, and hue to form a palette of colours to work from, then by mixing different strands of silk together, they are stitched in a variety of different ways to represent form, texture and surface. It is all done on an empty frame so that when the threads once woven together they form a canvas of pure silk with detailed scenery, nature and animals. They are designed to be hung so as to be viewed from both sides, so that light shines through which produces an extra effect of illumination, fish scales, waterfalls, clouds are all skilfully woven in a way that light will combine with the threads and bring it to life. It was a truly amazing labour of love; I was told some of these pictures took a whole year to complete with at least 3 people working on it together. I thought about everything I had seen, all the old architecture, the temples, the decorations, carvings and tried to think of anything modern that we produce today that has anywhere near the same amount of input, dedication and beauty. I could not think of any examples and realized that we don't seem to have the time any more. These days it seems it is maximum effect for the minimum time and effort.

I set my alarm for 5.00am because I decided paying the equivalent to 10 Euros a bit too much just to walk down a public road and onto a footpath to follow the tiger leaping gorge. They had set up a little toll booth further down the road at the end of the town, placed a barrier across the road and therefore I decided to get up early enough so that I could sneak past.

My alarm rang out but I was already awake. I find this happens most times when I set my alarm and I always awake just before it goes off, but I know if I did not set it I would probably sleep through, the act of setting an alarm seems to be like subconsciously writing a little memo in the boot sequence of the brain, must get up at 5 am it said.

It was still dark and very cold so consequently it took a bit of motivation to reach for the sleeping bag zipper,

"OK this time come on . . . . one two three . . . . now go for it . . . . Zzzzzzp" I launched myself out and proceeded to dance around hopping from one foot to the other on the freezing cold concrete floor, whilst simultaneously frantically grabbing at bits of warm clothing. Very soon I got my gear together and opened the door, it clunked and creaked open, shortly followed by a resonating echo which bounced around the stark, empty walls of the motel. Everywhere was completely black, no lights, nothing working. I did attempt to try to formulate some instructions to the owner when I checked in, with a mixture of hand signals and pointing at the clock, to try to explain that I wanted to leave very early in the morning. He had watched with enthusiasm as I attempted to communicate, grinning wildly he seemed to understand perfectly well that I had told him his motel was the best I had ever seen and that please could he send up a bottle of champagne along with the best prostitute in town and her sister at earliest possible convenience. As no prostitute arrived I realized at this point that he had not understood anything and it was probably a total lock down in which they would probably have locked the front door. I fumbled around for my headlamp and switched it on. I felt like a burglar and crept quietly down to explore the possibilities of a silent departure not wanting a confrontation whilst sneaking around and having to try to order any more unnecessaries.

Yes! as I suspected the front door was locked, but I remembered from the previous day that I had seen a door behind the reception that led into the kitchens, which I presumed led out into the back yard. An idea was forming and I promptly tried the kitchen door. The handle turned and I let out a sigh of relief that it was indeed unlocked, but the damn thing screeched noisily as I pushed the door open, "shit" I thought why is everything so deliberately noisy when you trying to sneak around, be quiet all of you. I quickly tried to compile some phrases in my mind in Chinese that I could use just in case the worst happened and I got ambushed by waiting ninjas, but it was too dark in there also and all I could remember in Chinese were a few random words: hello, bus, my, beautiful, chilli flower; from which no amount of creative anagrams or scrabble expertise could save my ass, besides my mind was not ready for anything complicated yet and all I could think about were those damn pink fluorescent chickens with red flashing eyes screeching, alarm, alarm, alarm!

The thought quickly ran through me that it might be funny to grab a few things to eat whilst I traversed the kitchen, but I decided better not to push my luck and instead cautiously tried the handle of the metal door at the back. Luckily again it was unlocked and I was out into the back yard and carefully edged my way around a corner to be faced with just one last obstacle. There were two huge metal gates and beyond that it led out into the street, but surely these will be chained and padlocked I thought to myself. I started to mentally prepare myself for some sort of stealth climbing, scaling up smooth steel gates with 23kilo of bag, shaking my head and thinking "why oh why do I get into these situations" I found a big bolt and latch that was keeping the gates shut and accepted the inevitable `clunk` blocked by some padlock or other device, but to my relief it opened and I was suddenly out and free. I felt as though I had survived some great mission and realised I had been holding my breath all the time, I sighed, then gulped in the crisp night air and with that objective completed I merrily set off down the road. Out into the crisp cold still of the night. My boots clumped heavily arousing the suspicion of elemental forces, dogs ears pricked up, noses sniffed the air until one by one they all joined in and the whole damn street was a snarling demonic canine concerto.

The snarling followed my progress house by house then eventually faded into the background as I left the urban sprawl and progressed towards the ticket booth. I quietly crept past, looking out for any more surprises and then beyond into a pitch black road. I stopped to retrieve a badly printed tourist map out of my bag, which supposed to show the start to the 'tiger leaping gorge' trail. The description and the printed 'map' was both as abstract as each other, with this and having to navigate in the dark it became a little disorientating.

In the description it described a school somewhere, then you were instructed to take a left turn just past the inky blob then just follow the trail . . . . yeah easy! Well I found the school, which it then said to go through, or past, or what I was not sure. I tried the gate to the school entrance but of course it was locked. I then searched around the buildings either side, suddenly a big dog jumped at the one entrance and started barking. I jumped backwards and my heart leapt into my mouth and decided not to go down that one. I searched around again and came across a side gate that was open with no dogs this time. I followed it which led around the side of a building to a wall which I climbed and then appeared outside what turned out to be the school toilets, "aaah yes good I am in" I thought

I was in a big open school yard unlit in total darkness. I wandered instinctively in the direction of uncertainty with just my headlamp lighting up a small circle of school yard ahead of me. I walked through as logically as I could trying to imagine where this path might start from, through the yard, through the basket ball yard, through the football pitch and then directly to a dead end, shit! I searched everywhere and could not find any trail . . . . just steep cliffs and dense vegetation to my left. Somewhere here the trail definitely almost maybe surely was supposed to start from; "it has to go up from here to the top of the ridge and then follows it east to the Gorge then turns northwards." I reasoned with myself.

Well I knew where I needed to be heading I just needed to find some sort of opening that would lead me up the steep slope to the ridge above. With that in mind I think my determination must have invented a small track, which I came upon and what looked like animal tracks that were going steeply up into the trees roughly in the right direction. There was not many other options available and I decided to follow them hoping even if this was not the right place then at some point I would intersect with the main trail higher up. I pushed my way through a small opening and started ascending up through dense trees and seemed to make good progress, it was still completely dark and no sound apart from my scrambling up through the undergrowth, getting snagged, breaking branches, which soon started to wear thin the sense of adventure, then suddenly I caught a glimpse up through the trees above me, eyes fully dilated marvelled at the twinkling stars raining down above me. I stopped to take it all in, the time, the place, the location, the strangeness of it all, this human being doing what I was doing that I recognize as me, I felt I was just occupying this body forcing it to do stupid things, like a driver would, somewhere within was me, the driver. Something felt so huge yet at the same time it was also infinitely microscopic. My mind tumbled into a black hole of infinite consciousness. I could almost see something, sense it and feel something so complete, so beautiful, and so mysterious, that it could not be know and was not allowed. Like trying to recall a dream that was so clear yet sometimes impossible to recall always just out of reach, some things just do not translate into conscious awareness. You can see it but not know it, yet you can know it but not see it, like the quantum particle which you can only detect its position or speed, never both at once. A paradox whereby I think God must have created a third particle so that the other two could be know, observed, and ultimately completely experienced. Things seem to happen in threes as they say; the holy trinity, the Vesica Pisces where two circles intersect and create a third, where edges meet, tangents coincide, vertices in geometry or nature a new environment is created, the magic number three, two particles that are deliberately collided annihilate and something new is born, a particle materializes and is suddenly able to have its position, speed and mass observable. I stopped to assess things here and thought about it all, it was the middle of the night and I was following what could be animal tracks up the side of a mountain with no idea of how where and why but somehow I knew it will all turn out fine. Quantum entangled, split and then settled down into full midnight mountain weirdness

Eventually higher up, the trail split into two then three and with the third addition it did join a better trail, a more defined path and as all paths must go somewhere I felt I was on my way. A little later there were cemented steps and the way became much more well trodden. I was feeling smug at this point thinking that as this must be the main trail now and my decision to be a bit reckless was a good one in the end. I continued ascending upwards for at least another 2 hours until eventually I was up out of the tree line and the extent and majesty of the clear sky was humbling, so many times having to stop, gaze and marvel at the stars, there were so many, so clear. I did not care now if I was in the right place or not because here and now I knew from the depths of my soul that I was in the right place and was now being rewarded with such a sight, filling my soul with freedom, joy and infinite knowingness. I was home again, finally in the arms of nature's infinite wisdom..

I reached a village much later which upon checking the vague descriptions in my tourist brochure it seemed to coincided with the description of the trail. I found a good vantage point to stop and rest for a bit and settled down for a spectacular breakfast show. I ate and watched peacefully as the sun rose, a new day, fresh. The shadows of the night crept back into the cracks of the earth. I love these moments these little treats these simple pleasures, to stop to rest to eat whilst watching the best visual dawn display than yesterday, amazing how it keeps coming up with new stuff and how many times you can see the same things yet be equally captivated by it. Mother nature surely is the ultimate artist.

I sat drinking my mug of tea and was feeling warm inside and smug that I had managed to bumble upon the trail; but that feeling soon turned to doubt as I continued along the way I noticed many faces looking at me in a way that bridges the gap of communication barriers. There is no need for language in these situations it is written across their faces . . . . `how did you get here and what the hell are you doing here kind of a look` I thought one man must have lost his chickens, as he was frantically pointing and sounding very annoyed about it all, but that is just their way I reassured myself. Chinese language all sounds a little over animated at times, with hints of frustration and aggression but I think they just want to know what, where, why and you really should not be going down here but be should really be going down there! It turned out that I was in fact going totally the wrong way and I was in the wrong place, because at some point a local man materialized who with an intense moment of animation, hand signals and determination soon put me right, but hey it all works out in the end. I do seem to be lucky like this and wonder if it is the same for everyone else, something always seems to turn up just at the right time just before I really make a big blunder, out of no where people will appear and something will prompt them to put me in the right direction. I am very grateful to whatever it is I need to be grateful to.

I walked for maybe an hour in the direction that was forcibly suggested by the little old man who had lost his chickens. Then later on I found a well marked trail that now had big bright yellow signs to follow so no way to get lost. Following this now took me on a journey of stunning dizzy views following a deep Gorge, far down below a white raging river could be seen the waters of which were draining down from high Himalayan mountains. I walked for 12 hours that day having the advantage of such an early start, being driven and tantalized by what was always just around the next turn, consequently I ended up finishing the whole walk in one long day, tired but completely satisfied I was very happy to come to rest at a guest house at the end of the trail which was run by a family of Tibetan origin. They were very friendly and very grateful for some customers at this quiet period of their winter season. I had not seen one tourist all day which had made for a very peaceful solitary walk and besides when it comes to nature I can be very selfish because I want to be alone with her.

Tietan Weddings And Wibbly Wobbly Worlds Wordsssssszzzzzz...

Chapter 7

I got talking to the owner who fortunately spoke quite good broken bad English, and told her my very loose travelling ideas and that I wanted to walk as much as possible, all the way if possible to Zongdian otherwise known as Shangri-La, a total of 120 km. The next village along they said was Haba village and told me of an interesting trail that you could take to walk there but said it was hard to find the way if you did know. I raised an eyebrow which was an indication that I was thinking, an potential adventure forming, then pleaded with them to draw a map for me so that I could try and find my own way. They seemed troubled by that but finally agreed and set about drawing me a map. I became excited about the prospect of following local trails which would take me away from the normal tourist routes and offer an elevated sense of adventure. I watched them eagerly and waited patiently for its completion. I watched and waited and waited; they scratched their heads, looked at each other, debated between themselves, argued an hen finally phoned a friend, they arrived, debated together, argued, drew bits, then frantically rubbed bits out, after literally 1 hour of this finally and with great pride, proudly showed me their hard efforts. I held this valuable bit of information in my hand and prepared myself to view a work of art, a detailed local map and hoped that it all made sense. I held it up and my jaw dropped in disbelief as in the end there was not too much to get confused or excited about. I struggled not to laugh, not wanting to offend their hard efforts and willingness to help me as they really tried hard and in the end I even think they enjoyed the challenge of it all, quite often in the past when I had stopped to ask directions and shown local people my map, they often took it and looked at it with a bemused blank expression and whilst starring at it upside down pointed me to the way I had just come, obviously not used to using them or even ever seeing one, and more importantly not wanting to lose face by admitting they did not know. Hence the invention of the Indian 'head wobble' which is perfectly neither yes or no, no way to lose face.

After 1 hour of combined effort they had produced a map which I could see they had thought about it really hard: they drew four big triangles, a snake chasing a tiger that was running away from spears that some demi God had sent raining down from heaven. I was not sure if this was some sort of representational historical map handed down from ancestors which was explaining the creation of heaven and earth, the location of the belly button of the world, or if they were just trying to challenge me at my own game of weirdness. I contained myself and asked if they could take me through it line by line, which they smiled proudly and proceeded to point at various bits describing what they represented, their explanation was even more abstract; they pointed at the triangles, space invaders and spiders and said that after two big mountains go left, then he pointed at the second big triangle, which now I was guessing that it was a mountain, so after the second big mountain go left . . . . long pause . . . . I thought he was going to start clearing his throat so I moved away a little.

. . . . Was he thinking?

no . . . .

That was it!

That was all!

That was the entire explanation, it was incredible the whole charade, the scribbling, rubbing out, the long debates, to finally come up with this, inside I was clawing around in my mind, hysterics at the madness of it all, it was in a way beautifully simple.

"Yes and? . . . ."

I was waiting for something else; "where's the village you talked about? How far was it from the second triangle, errr . . . . mountain I mean? What's the snake got to do with anything?"

My God I love it . . . . and I proudly kept it; completely useless as a map but it will remain a great source of amusement until the end of my days. With that I decided to hire the woman from the guest house instead and use her as a guide, but keep the map . . . . just in case?

The woman agreed to guide me after we negotiated a reasonable price which included being invited to and having to attend a wedding, from which afterwards she would be free of family matters to be able to guide me, so I was automatically invited to join them. After we could leave for Haba village, great why not I thought this will be interesting.

We got up very early to get ready and prepare for a walk up to a small village which was literally perched on the side of the mountain above us. We ate traditional Tibetan breakfast which included steamed bread and drank Tibetan tea of which I have come across before and knew what to expect, gradually since the first encounter of this beverage

I have actually slowly adapted and been able to swallow it, then after a few more attempts been able to keep it down, then more recently grown to actually enjoy it. Basically its tea; they put a little bit of tea in a big wooden tube, add hot water, Yak butter, salt, yes salt not sugar! Then mash it around with a big plunger that fits inside, a sort of Tibetian Expresso I suppose but without the delicious aroma of coffee and sweetness of sugar. I think I like and am fascinated with the whole process of it all more than the actual drinking of it, its like a little morning ritual, the preparation, the waiting, the gurgling, slurping sound as it got mixed and mashed with the plunger; a little cannabis this time went into the mix for some reason, why not a little twist for the wedding I guess. Then we all sat around a clay oven in their dark smoky kitchen, warming ourselves and hugging our tea. I looked at their smiling faces with fondness watching the steam from our cups engulf our smiles, what peaceful open people I thought to myself; I met them just yesterday but instantly feel so relaxed and can be myself around them, curious, interesting, and happy to be able to just sit not having or feeling the need to say anything.

The tea slid down like spent Dukhams Multigrade, leaving a trail of rich yak residue and cholesterol boost after burn, which left a very particular taste; a buttery residue which coated the entire inside of my mouth, throat, larynx then a sharp hit from the salt behind it all . . . . ping . . . . kind of wakes you up with a sort of slap round the face with a wet kipper whilst being insulted by your high school head master and his cane; and yes wakes you up and sets you up for the rest of the day, the philosophy of which is; if you can get this down you so early in the morning then you can handle pretty much anything else that the rest of the day may throw at you, my internal organs groaned slightly but any rebellious notions were muffled by a good coating of Tibetian tea. I was ready to go, I was ready for anything.

We set off taking a small track that led up behind the guest house up a steep mountain slope. She pointed to some small distant dwellings high up on the mountain side, "maybe 40 minutes" she said. Indeed we arrived 40 minutes later but sweating heavily now from the steep climb; the sun that had appeared above the eastern rocky horizon and the intensity pierced the surrounding landscape creating high contrast shadows and sharp detail for as far as the eye could see. The mornings and evenings were bitterly cold, freezing, minus double figures but as soon as the sun appeared it changed dramatically climbing quickly to up to 30 degrees at the peak of the day. The skin and complexion of people here took on a dark, leathery appearance and eyes adapted to the intense light were peering through extremely narrow slits.

We arrived at a house where many Tibetan people were gathering, their smiling faces, all dressed up in their brightly coloured traditional clothes, dazzling in these crystal clear conditions. More smiling faces as the amusement of a foreigner amongst them caught their attention but it was not over the top to make it uncomfortable, and they went about their wedding responsibilities. I joined in with a procession of people that was streaming into the courtyard of a house, passing by and being introduced to the bride and groom. I found a place to sit and then settle down amongst the crowd. I began scanning the variety of characters, the old, the young, women, children all have their own story I imagined and place amongst them all, much laughter continued through out it all and I was easily accepted amongst them.

I unpacked my camera discretely for not wanting to be intrusive and started to capture these faces and their individual stories that they provoked. I love the old folk here so rich are their faces all crinkled and marked but each line tells a story like the rings of the tree, a time, a place, religion, their faith, shining eyes that reach into your soul, "yes I can see you too my friend" as my eyes meet another, we peer into each other for some sort of exchange and I felt good.

Plates of food started to arrive and very soon tables everywhere were overflowing, excited hands picking up lovingly prepared food and still they kept coming back with more. I avoided drinking and refused anything alcoholic looking because I needed nothing and was enjoying the clarity of the moment. Someone came up to fill my cup that I was holding and I saw that it was a teapot, "aaaaaaah good . . . . tea" and offered up my cup smiling; a clear liquid came out, "oh . . . . water! why not" Thirsty from the salty food I downed it all in one go, maybe half a pint went down in big thirsty gulps until I felt the cold liquid try to evaporate from the depths of my stomach; as it left my cup and entered the warmth of my mouth, a mixture of high octane vapours and volatile liquid, gushed down my throat instantly removing the lining of Tibetan tea like paint stripper, to finally re-condense in my stomach; which then ignited and tried to make a fiery evacuation out through every orifice it could find. I contracted them all trying to contain the small nuclear explosion as every cell of my being chain reacted. I still had a mouthful of the stuff left that I could not quite swallow; Looking around I could see no option desperately trying to remain composed but my red eyes gave it away a bit that were now bulging under the pressure, streaming with tears and purple faced; much to the amusement of my hosts I held my nose closed my eyes and swallowed again . . . . kaboooom! for a split second I was not sure if I was going to throw up or die right there on the spot; for the next five minutes my heart was beating through my chest my temples pounding and I could feel the blood pumping hard around my body, then slowly but surely as the alcohol saturated my being, red blood corpuscles started dancing merrily with white blood corpuscles and all became oblivious to their gender, colour, DNA sequence, or more importantly which direction they were just going, consequently the lack of cellular coordination and the high altitude lack of oxygen, my head jumped three meters to one side and my brain the opposite direction. All fears of embarrassment suddenly sprouted wings and flew out the window of responsibility, gliding on the thermal differences of the Himalayan festivities, and all suddenly became quite pleasant and surreal.

This stuff should come with a class A warning.

Hmmmmm very nice, very relaxed now, smiling giggling laughing, and wobbling a lot; for the rest of the day I wandered around in a dream like grinning fool stupor, enjoying the sensation of being, relaxed, happy and . . . . completely absolutely drunk, along with most of the other men it seemed as I leered around, who had also been downing this fire water, not just sipping it respectfully but competing with each other in very loud macho drinking competitions. At some stage I think I must have got abducted; I certainly lost my guide; I definitely lost my mind and kind of woke up suddenly realizing that I was inside someone's house talking with an old toothless guy; well he was babbling away in Tibetan, I was picking up bits and pieces asking what this is? What's that? Who am I . . . . ? from which they seemed to take great pleasure and enjoyed telling me everything in their strange tongue. I was not sure how many hours or days for that matter that I had been doing this, but eventually I was discovered by and retrieved by the geust house owner; I think she had taken me to her parents house for `safe keeping` and now instructed me that it was time to go back down . . . .

"oh yeah, that's it I remember now we have to go back down to lower world . . . . woo hoo come on lets gooooooo"

I was very enthusiastic about it all but I could just not understand it, it was so difficult to walk, and down, very, very steeply down . . . .

"bloody hell I am flying woooooosh . . . down, so far down there, weeeeeeeee, whoooops"

She grabbed me from behind again and told me to please be careful, she had a good grip though, drunk as I was and pretty numb to everything I can still remember the sensation of strength that she had, grabbing my arm time and time again, patiently telling me to be careful. I totally trusted her, I felt safe, invincible, but still very very drunk on this Tibetian fuel injected mountain rocket fuel.

I had an outstanding day with them all and the evening continued back at the guest house with much talking laughing and dancing, they put on some Tibetian music for me, it is their main form of entertainment and love to sing and dance. I was still feeling very light headed still and happy but sober enough by now to still be aware of my inability to dance in any way; I had the grace of a cabbage someone had once informed me, but they kept insisting that I take to the floor. Finally I suggested that I would be more inspired to make a fool of myself if they were to dress up in their traditional costumes and then we could all dance together, they thought that was a great idea and promptly went off to get changed. It was not long after they returned completely transformed in brightly adorned outfits, head dresses grinning from ear to ear and handed me my outfit, what the hell is this I thought and obediently put on what they gave me. I was sporting a similar Tibetan dress full with head-dress and proceeded to dance, we laughed and joked all night. Much later on after finally finding my bed I lay there for a moment thinking of the past few days, weeks and events, and again smiled thinking 'I did not think I was going to be doing this today'

I slept then I woke but wished I had not; I felt like a military parade, parts of me kept falling out, my brain, my eyes, my mouth, euuuugh what happened,

"you idiot you got drunk again" The guardian angel scolded . . . . I warned you not to do it, just like before and just like last time . . . . I often have these debates with myself maybe it makes me feel that I am in a relationship and reminds me what I am not missing,

"Yeah, yeah stop nagging I know it" I replied nursing my pounding temples.

High octane breath, heady fumes of fermented rice and body odour of a festering Yak was going to be the theme to the rest of the day. I felt in a complete mess along with a slightly semi-detached feeling of body and mind. Not even the Tibetan tea managed to kick me into shape that morning and disguise the alcohol taste; I belched and burped alcohol fumes all day, moaned and groaned as we set out off along the trail to Haba village. This was going to be a matter of endurance, stamina and I was regretting the festivities of the night before, knowing the beauty of this day would pass me by.

The crisp morning air and elevated scenery took my mind off my condition for a while as we climbed high up over a pass to the north, through trees and wilderness, yes I was grateful that she was with me guiding the way and not having to think was a huge relief. Today there was no way I would have found the way in this condition and the trail was non existent in places you really did just have to know. Towards the top I saw a distant mountain peak covered in snow at the summit, wind was blowing a whisp of snow from its summit; it looked impressive and beautifully prominent against the backdrop of clear blue sky. I enquired to my guide as to what mountain it was, she told me

"That Haba snow mountain"

She said and that she had climbed it.

"Ah ha tell me more about it" I asked her, my interest suddenly stimulated and interested in living again. She said it was a hard climb but nothing too technical providing weather is good, it was 5400 meters, a little bit big for a first climb I thought. I had never been so high before only in the Pyreneese which I had climbed just over 3000 meters. I was quickly going through in my mind all the pros and cons, but already I knew what the next potentially stupid thing I would be compelled to try and do. It remained with us for the rest of the walk the backdrop to my desires.

Six hours later we arrived in Haba village, very relieved to finally arrive after walking off one of the worst hangovers in history. I paid my guide for her trouble, thanked her and hoped to see them again someday. It had felt like a never ending day fighting a huge desire to just find a sunny spot and hibernate. My mind and my soul were still traumatized from the wedding of which certain parts of me I was sure were permanently left behind there.

It was a small village consisting of just a few buildings which were scattered either side of a straight road. I came across a guest house, quickly signed myself in and threw my rucksack down on the floor of my room. I slumped on my bed; relieved my eyes of their duty and allowed my mind to flat-line for a moment . . . . whoosh . . . . sounds distanced themselves as dream time and reality overlapped. I sunk inside myself as the world retracted and nothingness engulfed me, somewhere I was revelling in the stillness of it all, and nothingness was quite exquisite.

After returning from oblivion and feeling like living again I went back to the reception to make enquiries about the mountain. The owner, a middle aged Tibetan woman, told me that she had climbed it many times and talked fondly about it with a spiritual passion. I replied that I was really interested to climb it myself, and her mood suddenly took on a darker tone as she realized I was tapping her for some information so that I could climb it alone, or I thought maybe she was hoping for a little business and was trying to set me up with guides, yaks and porters, which was not my scene and certainly well out of my budget range. Eventually she gave in to my persistent questions about the mountain and wanting to know as much as possible about it. I think I got my point across that I was not just recklessly satisfying a macho ego. I wanted to know as much as possible so to be safe, the approach, the level of difficulty, and slowly she understood my passion also and that I really wanted to attempt it safely. She changed her mood a bit and started to give away a few directions and information. I guess for safety reasons it was wise for her to tell me all that she could. She motioned me to follow her outside and from there we both stood and looked up at this stunningly beautiful mountain that was dominating the background. She pointed to a patch of ground high up where there were no trees.

"there" she pointed

"You have to get to there"

With a snake like motion of her hand and with broken English I gathered it was sort of up and over the ridge then round and follow the tree line up, or she was making some kind of Chinese dragon magic, either way I was very much entranced by it all. I thought about it for a moment, but then decided against asking her if she could draw a map for me, and instead thanked her. I went back inside and started looking at all the collection of photographs taken with various people who had been to the top, various alpine images lined the walls, mountaineers fully equipped with cramp-ons, ice axe, goggles, roped together ascending up into the thin upper atmosphere, some were in full blizzard conditions, and the seriousness of it all really started to sink in, wondering if I was trying to bite off a bit more that what I could chew this time; also bit worried about acclimatization having no experience how I would feel at these altitudes. I resided myself to just take it easy and go as far as I thought was reasonable and felt safe, just try it and maybe the conditions will be good, maybe the way up will be easy to spot as you approach it, maybe dragons will swoop down! Those rose coloured glasses tinted everything a hopeful hue.

It was a perfect full moon that night which cast a mystical magical blanket over the landscape; the mountain stood out in full monochrome and looked as though it had been airbrushed by some science fiction artist. I felt energized, excited, nervous and extremely restless. My mind was going over everything: was I in good condition? Did I have all the information I needed? What equipment should I take? I came to the conclusion I would probably not be conditioned enough and it would be tough. The highest I had ever climbed was earlier on that same year whilst in the Pyrenees with a good friend of mine who had been crossing the entire range following the HRP (high route Pyrenees) we walked maybe three weeks together and climbed three of the highest peaks, the highest of which was 3400 meters, so although relatively fit and healthy the altitude was probable going to be a problem. After some more internal debate I thought it would be interesting to try it anyway and if it got too hard or dangerous then just let it go and accept it as a good conditioning walk. I decided to do it, then some time later I decided not to do it, stir-frying doubt and ideas on a full moon lit night until my mind was burnt to a crisp in a mystical syrup of danger, adventure and doubt, and with that I suddenly felt completely fatigued, drained and trudged of to my room and hoped sleep would smooth out any conflicting doubt and the morning rays of sunlight restore the balance of adventure to more favourable heights.

I got up to go to the toilet which was outside and I had to cross a courtyard. The air was intensely cold and crisp; it had been gradually getting colder and colder each day as I made my way further north and the elevation now was at 2300 meters. I looked up at the perfectly clear sky like I had just seen it for the first time, drawn in by it all and then humiliated by her mind numbing vastness of stars; I was suddenly projected within the cosmos but my mind started struggling, trying to hang on somewhere impossible, teetering on the edge of our spiral galaxy, and just about to lose my grip from the gravitating pull of the infinite abyss beyond into unobservable space, where even the most far reaching algebraic expressions could not quantify. I gazed transfixed to it all. Under this incredibly bright full moonlight night which perfectly coincided with this very moment to illuminate the snowy peak of the mountain that I was in obviously still in full debate with, it was very much still taunting me.

"Look how beautiful I am" It provoked me . . . . yes it did look absolutely stunning, silent, harmless, peaceful and how close it seemed, tempting me to test the illusion to reach out and touch it, yes so tantalizingly close and irresistibly beautiful, but beauty has a price my guardian angel reminded me, and the serpent spoke beneath the flower,

"Can you resist, can you resist me?"

Suddenly a shooting star streaked across the entire skyline from one side to the other, seemingly at just the right moment just to super enhance what was already too speechless to think about, my mind crash landed back on Terra fir-ma and made me forget what it was that I nearly thought about. I let it go like a dream that you feel was so beautiful but not allowed to remember in waking life. What an amazing world this is I thought to myself and took it all as a good omen for tomorrow. I was suddenly filled with awe, inspiration, confidence and indulged myself with a little superstition that the heavens had blessed me; even if I don't get to the top it will still be worthwhile I continued to assure myself, life will come out from hiding and meet me half way.

In the morning I felt completely refreshed and charged with divine confidence. I eagerly set off from the village and very soon came upon a trail that seemed to be going in the basic direction I wanted and following it as far as I could with my eyes; it did seem to head towards the patch of open ground high up on the mountain where the woman had described I should get to. I continued on for about two hours walking past small settlements then out into a forest, where within were criss-crossed with small trails, with no land mark and being boxed in all around with trees, I did my best to maintain my desired direction until I came across a major fork in the trail; the left seemed to be going down to a big dry river bed and the other straight up which I would have thought to be the good direction of up; normally I get some sort of instinctive feeling and go by a gut feeling, but this time I stopped and could not feel anything my brain said up but everything else kept quiet, maybe I was in a sort of human GPS black spot and the feeling of you're getting lost aren't you! came over me. I had already walked quite a few hours of instinctive path finding and lost count of how many forks, spoons and dinner parties I had missed, so the possibility of 'lost' was probably high, and now, definitely I felt it for the first time that nagging voice of doubt, then hesitation as an internal debate erupted. I really did not want to lose time back tracking, and the ego fighting me not wanting to be wrong and having to back track.

I looked around hoping to find some sort of a sign, some inspiration, and then noticed an old man sitting on a rock perfectly in the fork of the road where I had just been standing. Eh! . . . . I was sure he was not there before, I would have noticed him, there seemed to be no houses around and no reason for him to be there apart from waiting for me to arrive maybe! As I approached him he did not seem to notice me or even to be surprised

"nee how" Hello I said and pointed up to the mountain making a mountain shape with my hands and a walking motion with my fingers, he grinned wildly nodding and replied in perfect Engrish . . . .

"ahhh good, good, yes, you go that way not this way no good, no good that way"

Pointing to the right trail that my brain earlier wanted to take, which went deeper upwards into the forest getting more and more lost no doubt. I took his advice and proceeded down to the river and looked for a place to cross. Again it was perfect timing I think I would have chosen the other way if forced to make a decision, and maybe would have taken me well out of my way, got lost, frustrated and lose a lot of time and energy. He seemed to have been waiting for my arrival and now happy to have served his purpose, promptly disappeared again.

I picked up a bigger trail on the other side of the river, well trodden, with what I presumed were yak hoof prints, chocolate wrappers that I presumed had been mindlessly discarded by tourists and had served to mark the way for me, this must be the main trail I thought. I followed it up and eventually it came to the area of cleared trees. I lost the trail again as all tracks diverged and took some time before coming across a small opening and then more hoof prints appeared. I followed them again and slowly it started to become much more steep, twisting, zig zagging around boulders and exposed tree roots that the traffic of heavy laden beasts had unearthed. The tree line continued upwards, which had me clambering up over more boulders, until eventually I emerged on top of a craggy ridge that allowed a brief glimpse into the valley below, which now was just a hazy mirage of the village that I had started out from early this morning. Already it was all looking and feeling quite elevated here, but a deep knowing of so much more to come welled up inside me; I could feel its presence, its eyes, or whatever it was that it was using to follow my progress and to perceive me, it was everywhere, its eyes were everywhere and yet no where, but somewhere above it was waiting, momentarily obscured by the dense forest ahead. I continued following this ridge that had been steadily ascending for some time and started to notice a definite shortness of breath; I looked at my altimeter which now read 3800 meters, already more than I had been before and therefore slowed down to pace myself. I had been walking a good 4 hours now and was starting to feel the weight of my rucksack, as the oxygen became thinner so did everything else start to feel heavier and harder. My pace became slower and slower as the fatigue worsened with the increasing altitude until finally I was finding myself having to stop every 12 paces or so, then remain standing there gasping for air until my breathing became steady again. It felt very strange, new sensations that I had not come across before a conflict of mind and body; my legs felt great, had power and wanted to go much quicker but I just could not regulate my breathing and I had a sensation that my mind had jumped out of my skull and was reeling a few feet above myself in light headed spasms; my temples started to ache and systematically pounded with every beat of my heart. I thought I was starting to ascend the various stages of classic altitude sickness and was wondering at what stage or base camp I was at, and when unconsciousness would overcome me. A small army of confrontation sized up to one another, ego on one side and fear on the other, each wanting the other to change his mind and turn around This was no time for such a battle, so I forced myself to relax and slow down even more, placing one foot in front of the other slowly and methodically plodding upwards. Still the sensations increased, regularly misplacing my footing, stumbling and feeling dizzy, slightly drunk, and off balance. I was now at 4000 meters and I had walked directly 1700 meters up from where the village was. The tree line had thinned out now and I started to see much more patches of ice, hugging the crevices and shaded areas.

Then suddenly as I turned the next corner, the snowy peak of Haba Snow mountain majestically appeared. I had not seen a glimpse of it for some time being obscured by the trees and then suddenly it was there looking down on top of me appearing to be so close. It was strange I was almost disappointed as it looked too easy to reach the summit now, an attachment with the goal, with a feeling of not wanting the adventure to end just yet by reaching the final goal, what you want, what you desire does not satisfy you completely when you have it, it is all temporary, there will be a new mountain to climb after this one, then another, higher, harder, better, always trying to at least match the sensation before if not exceed it, the phrase kept coming to mind "you don't need to climb a mountain to know how high it is"

It was an uplifting moment though and new energy surged through me; I felt like I could have dropped my heavy bag there and then and made a dash for the summit, but in reality it was still another 1400 meters higher up, it was the crystal clear sub zero atmospherics that made everything look so close and temptingly accessible.

I stopped at a clearing that looked nice and flat and protected from wind, so decided it would be a good place to stop and to set up my little solitary 'base camp' so I eagerly set about the task, but I soon discovered that by just unpacking my sleeping bag took an enormous effort just to pull it out of its cover. I started laughing at how feeble I felt, and even that outburst cut the comedy short and had me gasping for air again. I had to stop to catch my breath several times as everything was ten times harder than normal. This was exhausting and I imagined what it would be like another 1400 meters higher?

My temples still felt sore with a sort of bruised feeling, and a constant pressure inside of them that was not quite breaking out into a full blown headache but the potential was there. Already this was the highest I had ever been and the real climb had not even begun yet. I clambered out of my tent and scanned the peak above me. I could see the top easily and I tried to pick out which way looked best, from here I was hoping to see some marks, some trails but it all looked perfectly white. After setting up camp I followed the trail a little further up to see the way ahead for tomorrow and came upon a stone building where a group of Chinese people were standing about. I went up to them to introduce myself and luckily found one of them who was able to speak English; I learnt that they were heading up to the top planning to start very early in the morning and had hired some local guides. We got talking a little more and told them I had hoped to find my own way up at which they shook their head and spoke with one of the guides who then offered for me to follow them up, this is perfect I thought and was starting to see a plan finally come together with the certainty now of getting to the top with safety on my side.

I was invited to spend the evening with them and as darkness started descending along with it came the plummeting temperature. I nodded with enthusiasm at the thought of four walls, a roof, and probably a nice warm fire. I quickly thanked them all and agreed to come back to stay with them for the evening.

I returned sometime later to their shelter; It was a small rustic stone building with a very low roof just tall enough for small oriental folk to feel comfortable in and which made me much taller than I wasn't. I pushed open the heavy wooden door and peered through the smoky haze; sure enough a large central fire was ablaze and I could see many faces that were shimmering orange and red all sat around its perimeter. I introduced myself to them all one by one; happy glances and curious smiles exchanged and I bounced a few questions around to see who was the easiest person to understand; luckily most of them could understand me providing I talked slow and kept it simple. We ate a simple meal; some sort of broth made from a combined effort of what people had with them and noodles of course. Very soon we were talking and laughing together like old friends. I could not believe I was here and how lucky I was that it had all turned out the way it had so far. Tears were rolling down my cheeks not out of joy but from the smoke and soon became too unbearable so I made my excuses to leave and agreed a time to rendezvous with them in the morning.

I went back to my tent and settled down for the night. Although very tired I had very little sleep as it was extremely cold after seeing my thermometer drop down to—8 inside my tent. I struggled to relax thinking too much about the climb, the anticipation of it all and also I had a constant uncomfortable feeling with my breath; it did not feel natural any more like I had to concentrate, a sort of claustrophobic feeling. I did some scuba diving once and a similar feeling came to mind of having to suck slightly harder than normal before the air valve would activate then you would suddenly get a gulp of air under a pressure that you were not naturally accustomed to, it was like that and therefore very hard to breath normally and relax.

I went in and out of sleep ll night until I finally gave up, sat up and switched off my alarm prematurely. 3.00am I was awake and eagerly wanted to get going. I heard movement outside in the distance so quickly got dressed wanting to be out there and join in with the preparations. I put on my layers then darted out from my tent. I was ready to go . . . .

"come on guys I am ready lets go, what are you doing messing around still?"

I paced about for some time, wondering when the action would start and in the end waited nearly 2 hours watching these guys prepare themselves. I thought it was going to be a precise assault on the summit; I was all fired up eager to learn from the experience of these local guides, but very quickly I learned what the morning's priorities were and why they had opted for such an early alarm call. I had to remind myself that these guys were not like me, they were Chinese first, then mountaineers and anyway I was just tagging along and needed to be patient. I watched bemused and waited for them until they finished their ritual equivalent of our full English breakfast which consisted of cooking noodles, chopping vegetables, seasoning and regularly tasting until it was suitable enough for their palette. Finally after what seemed like hours of preparing and cooking food then followed a frantic 5 minutes of slurping, spitting, burping and farting. Only then were they ready enough to getting their gear together, which I thought they would have done night before, and now looking lost and confused at which bits they needed and which bits were missing out of their kit. I started to realize that many of them have not done this before, and were looking quite unprepared as I caught sight of pair of skateboard knee pads that one of them were wearing! Motorbike gloves and ray bans. They were happy enough though, enthusiastic and we were going to the top.

This was it, the guides gave a few final rounding up orders and set off ahead, then systematically the others got going one by one following each other out into the darkness. slowly a line of headlamps snaked through the darkness, up into the crisp morning mountain air under a bright moon and a canopy of unhindered twinkling lights from distant stars. Deafening silence was suddenly pierced with the sound of multiple crampons piercing the brittle snow, which were producing a brittle, metallic squeaking, creaking sound, screeeek screeek screeek, unique mountain music which was to be the mantra that will follow us to the top. It was a steep climb right from the start and it never really gave out to anywhere flat, and although now carrying very little weight with just a light bag that had a few extra layers and provisions, it gradually got harder and harder. At 4800 meters I found I had very little energy to spare, my untrained oxygen starved muscles were at full operating capacity, it was like being a snail in a snail marathon race; to an outsider it looked like we were not making any effort at all but in fact we were flat out and rapidly heading for the finish line extremely slowly.

I was placing each foot slowly and steadily one in front of the other, concentrating hard not to misplace my footing, not to exert any unnecessary energy and therefore the next few hundred meters went accordingly slow. We reached 5000 meters and I stopped to acknowledge the achievement and looked at the positions of everyone else in their own various stages of personal triumph or torture maybe. One of the guides that was just below me soon caught up and overtook me, puffing away on a cigarette, he cheerily waved at me, stopped to say hello and to see if I was alright, then took another long pull on his cigarette and promptly strode upwards seemingly without any effort or shortness of breath! Amazing.

The air here now in this alpine pre dawn was biting cold like I had never felt before; I looked down at my altimeter the temperature read—20 and with the wind that was picking up now was bringing the wind chill down even further suspecting that I could have added another—10 to that. I had some good layers of clothing though, a fleece and finally a down jacket which I then had to add another layer of protection by taking out a waterproof jacket out of my rucksack to stop the intense wind chill that was managing to penetrate through all these layers. My hands and feet were also getting a bit numb now and so I diverted my attention to the task at hand and continued upwards, taking my attention back to walking and concentrating on putting one foot in front of the other; each step I took reminding myself that it was that little bit closer to the final goal.

"You don't have to climb the mountain to know how high it is, but if you do you never forget." I revised and repeated to myself.

Soon the first rays of morning light appeared on the eastern horizon and slowly, eerily the third dimension of form, shape and distance illuminated into view. I could now see a well defined layer of cloud just below where I presumed our little base camp was. I was looking out over a horizontal plane of cloud ocean that seemed to go on forever, a stratospheric ocean of cloud and imagined how amazing this was going to look from the top having the advantage of a 360 degree panorama. I looked up towards the prize, and yes . . . . there it was, just up there and now only about another 400 meters. My temples had developed a steady beat now and were doing some kind of percussion with the beat of my heart and placement of feet which from time to time sent my head spinning. I could only manage to walk about 6 paces then needed to stop to catch my breath again, rasping at the intense freezing air. Ice had formed a thick layer on my moustache, eyebrows, eyelashes and stalactites of nose sculpture gravitated towards the earth which systematically broke off. My face was hurting earlier but now was relieved of any pain by the numbing effects of the cold. I tried to imagine how these early attempts on Everest must have been like at that time with their heavy, basic, cold equipment, frostbite, storms and at nearly another 4000 meters higher than where I currently was, it was just impossible to imagine. Already this felt like I had been walking constantly and nearly vertically upwards for days, with all the previous day and now at least another 5 hours and still going up.

I could now see the last 150 meters where the route curved its way up forming a crest of very steep, shiny wind polished ice that shimmered like water, directly to the left hung huge ice forms that bent and curled over, pointing downwards like huge white serpent fangs into a void that sent my mind reeling with vertigo. I was so near to the top, with just this last obstacle to traverse made of wind swept, polished ice. I approached it nervously sensing a certain seriousness, a heaviness, a kind of cruel unforgiving entity was waiting for me to see how I would react. It rose up like a huge wave on which I would have to walk on its crest. When I was within reach I tested the new surface with my cramp on; I had this sensation that it would just glance off it like the ground was made of pure quartz and would not hold my weight on such a crazy incline. I dramatically dug in the front of my boot, the two spikes stuck in hard and anchored my feet perfectly giving me the confidence I was hoping for and consequently pushed hard on my legs to start this last ascent. The increased incline was torturous on my ankles, and my calf muscles that felt like they were going to pop. With each step I was having to dig in hard with the tips of my boots, balance and push up from there, each foot one by one into the ice and slowly ascend. About half way I felt completely at the mercy of nature; if anything happens here I have no option but to learn to fly; to my left I was aware of but did not really dare to entertain it too long by looking a it, out the corner of my eye I could see an icy lip as the crest curled over like a breaking wave, sending the mind out over the edge into an awaiting void. My temples were really pounding now, muscles bursting, systematically placing one foot in front of the other trying not to exert too much effort and get out of rhythm until slowly it started to flatten out a little, an instant relief to be walking on the soles of my feet again, steadily plodding on and occasionally looking down where a few of the others were still small figures slowly pacing upwards. I looked up and could wee one of the guides was already at the top and taking out another cigarette; a puff of white smoke streaked from his mouth as the charging wind snatched it away, and slowly but surely he became closer and closer then with the last few paces I staggered up towards him. My legs were shaking like jelly and gasping for air again with the surge of excitement. I managed to let out a few short bursts of exclamations, a freezing numb triumphant melange of slurring, swearing and desperately trying express something unexspressable. I was Euphoric and then lost all rhythm the smallest emotional outburst caused me to gasp and pant for a few minutes. I beamed instead and shook the hand of the guide, thanked him with my eyes for such an unforgettable experience; beneath his mirrored goggles I could see a glint of knowingness and was equally humbled even after maybe doing the same climb countless times. This infinite substance of nature.

I regained my composure slightly and stopped swaying from side to side quite so much and marvelled at the 360 panorama of cloud sea; pyramids of rock pierced, or floated, or levitated upon the layer of cloud below. Numb, stunned, exited, cold, tired I did not care really how my body felt; I was intoxicated with a sensory overload of relief, joy, amazement and visual candy of the moment. The weather had been very kind and I was unbelievably very lucky to have such favourable conditions; to have found these people to follow up and thankful to my own body for getting me there to the top.

We did not spend too long at the top, for one reason it was extremely cold and it seemed we had only had a small window of opportunity, for as the sun rose so the thermals shifted, and the wind quickly increased to the point of feeling the need to start crawling on hands and knees, also the intensity of the sun started to melt the ice. This was where things start to change unfavourably very quickly and where so many accidents occur in the mountains, because of bad timing then getting stranded and exposed with escalating conditions, melting ice causing instability and of course rapidly fading energy, drained by the cold and the exertion of getting to the top, it was not over yet, there was still a long way down and equally painful for unconditioned 'down muscles'.

We all started back down and I took position in the middle of them all keeping my distance in case of a fall, ideally we should have been roped up together but they did not seem to have any, or thought they did not need to maybe, but it is easy to become complacent after climbing the same mountain a few times I supposed, that is when nature will often give you a slap to remind you who is boss. I started to notice one of the guys just below me stumbling quite a lot, obviously tired by now and struggling more and more to stop his legs collapsing under him. Then suddenly I see him stumble and dropped down again, but this time it looked more 'heavy' as though he had just been shot in the head, his body just sort of 'slumped' then a cloud of white exploded as he tumbled head over heals picking up momentum very quickly, his legs and arms thrashed about loosely like a rag doll. His bag flew off in the air along with various other bits of equipment which tumbled and fragmented, until finally he himself came to a stop in a contorted pile of snow and limbs. I froze watching in disbelief as he lay there motionless.

"shit he's dead" I thought, it was a hell of a tumble and I rewound the sequence in my mind seeing his head making contact with the ground, compacting and then being throw around again in another full circle.

I tried as quickly as I could to get to him whilst making sure I did not make the same dramatic descent. Upon reaching him I could see that he was already stirring, relieved but still concerned as I was sure he must have broken every bone in his body. Then he was motionless and made no attempt to move, the wind was certainly completely knocked out of him, but his eyes were rolling around and seemed to be coming in and out of consciousness. I spoke to him, "take it easy, don't try to move you are OK don't worry" He started to focus on me and tried to formulate words, but he looked and sounded like one of my recent Tibetan wedding adventures, slurring and babbling incoherently.

Miraculously there seemed to be nothing broken apart from a bit of pride and ego. I looked at his skate boarding knee pads that were now down by his ankles and smiled, maybe they helped after all I thought to myself. We found and gathered his things together then helped him to his feet; he was not a big man but now he seemed to gravitate heavily at least twice the weight that he actually was, bearing down on my shoulders with the burden of extreme fatigue. I carried him the rest of the way down with the help of one of the other guides.

After what seemed like another torturous few hours slowed down even more with our casualty, we arrived back at base camp and I left them there so that I could gather my tent and equipment together. Inside my tent I laid down and rested; my temples were pounding worse than ever. I was exhausted inside and out but my mind would not rest, it was over stimulated above and beyond trying to recollect the events of the past day or two. I could not believe I stumbled upon this mountain and had already climbed it. I was revelling with satisfaction after completing what I felt was such a big event and had now appeased some primordial need that my soul had hungered for. It was still early days though, just the first month of my travels and already I felt I was on bonus time. Thank you Universe.

I returned sometime later packed and ready to make the way down to the village. I said my farewells to the rest of them and was given a business card by the guy I had helped; he said that if I ever needed a place to stay that he has a guest house back in Dali where I had come from, he urged me to come and visit him and to stay as long as I wanted free of charge; had it been northwards I would have surely taken him up on his kind offer, but mostly I was relieved he was OK, smiling much more now and certainly a little bit more humble than before.

I walked back down to the guest house that same day and a new release of energy sort of came surging back, with the increased oxygen as I descended I could feel new power and energy coming back into my legs and amazing new lung capacity. I felt like a gazelle, light, powerful with a playful spring in my step that urged me on. It was a hell of a long day, 9 hours this morning to the summit and back then another 5 hours to the village, a healthy 14 hour walk, which my legs and my body felt completely detached by the time I got there. I was completely done, finished, nothing left, what a great day.

Subsequently I slept very well that night, short but a kind of deep sleep so deep that I am sure I disappeared and then re invented myself in the early hours of the morning. I find this that the more you push yourself the less you seem to need sleep; I woke early, sprang up out of my bed and felt totally alive, invincible . . . . tingling all over with new boundaries breeched, cellular rejuvenation and what felt like a new re organization of resources, and cleansing of body and mind, literally all the shit scared and exhilarated out of me! overnight my body had sold out, liquidated and then merged with a new manufacturer metamorphosis from fiat 126 to a Ferrari . Vroooom . . . . I was ready to hit the road again and on to seek the legendary Shangrilla.

I headed off towards the next village, Bashotai which was a 30 km hike. I had no choice but to follow the road and had ran out of local currency so could not hop on to a bus even if I wanted to. The last of my currency I gave to the guide for his help. Did not matter; money had no bearing on the way I felt at the moment. I was still on a high from the achievement yesterday and settled down to a steady days hike along the road ready to face whatever came my way. I stopped just short of the next village, my legs were complaining finding the tarmac tedious to walk on and they did not want to go any further. I agreed with them they had done very well the last day or so, therefore decided to make camp on a hill amongst what looked like a grave yard. Nearby were running water and a great view of the valley to the east, thinking the sun will be up early from this point and warm everything up in the morning. With that I made camp amongst the dead and made a fire, cooked and enjoyed my solitude amongst these dead and I felt so alive.

I had a disturbed sleep but not due to any discontented spirits though; I still had the remains of the chest infection that I picked up whilst in Bangkok, literally big lumps of that place kept coming up, and found myself coughing and hacking most of the night. I guess I had been spoilt from the clean air of southern France where I had been spending much of my time.

Next day I continued following the road, which tediously climbed slowly upwards 700 meters, it was a marathon of tarmac that took many hairpin twists and turns that I desperately searched for any chance to cheat them by taking short cuts through the rough landscape around. I managed to find a few trails that cut through the switch backs and shortened the road work considerably. The road dropped down again the other side then it rose up again winding upwards another 1000 meters, making progress but I was fading fast, this place and the tarmac was hard on the legs.

It was midday and I wanted to stop, I was hungry, tired and felt the need to just lie down and sleep. Just at that point I saw a group of Chinese that were working just off from the side of the road cutting trees, our eyes met and they waved, signalling me to come over and making hand signals to eat. I hesitated just long enough to make a few calculations and decisions battling with mind, body and stomach, the stomach finally got the majority of the vote as always, but I was relieved to have this opportunity to stop and rest. I went over to them and gave quick introductions enough to tell them I was tired, hungry and on my way walking to Shangri-La. They smiled and without hesitation offered me tea, Tibetan tea, but this time the butter and the richness of it was very welcome; I could feel my body absorbing and processing all the fats and salt, ahhhhhhh the warmth of the fire also was exquisite, hot liquid to drink then eating Tibetan bread and soup, which was a broth made from vegetables and yak meat, pretty old by the texture and smell of it and mainly just fat and gristle, but even this was a rich and much needed meal compared to the rations I had been eating, which had consisted of muesli or noodles. I looked around at them individually and they seemed to have no more interest to know anything else, just very content with my presence, nothing else to say but to enjoy the moment. After sharing the food and the fire it left me feeling warm inside and out; my cheeks were glowing and the drone of their incoherent chattering started to hypnotise me and I could feel sleep wanting to envelope me, like a drug it permeated through me until it was impossible to fight it; the sounds became distant and echoey and the intoxicating effects of sleep pulled heavily on my eyelids and started to close. I did not fight it and laid down listening to the crackling of the fire. I felt as though I was completely wrapped in cotton wool. The voices got more distant and unimportant, a moment seemed to pass, then I spoke something which made me jump out of a deep crevasse that I had fallen into, a deep part of the subconscious and slipped away, just a few seconds I think but so, so far away, the jolt back to waking reality was a shock; I think I must have jumped and felt my heart miss a beat, then as I regained stability to where, who, why, when I let go again . . . . just ten minutes or so but slipped into such a deep place and I had gone. I love this sort of tiredness one that I remember as a child after an exciting youthful day full of play, discovery, imagination and adventure, an innocence, a purity, sleep that we used to do as a child in the back of the car driving home from a long summers day out and our minds so free of clutter, so open, so free, so innocent we sleep deep

I suddenly heard myself snoring and woke up to catch the end of the last gargling noise I was making, then I looked around at my friends who were smiling and I nodded and laughed. How safe and comfortable I thought.

My energy quickly restored I thanked them and got going again, feeling totally great again. It was 2.30 pm and I was thinking I would not be able to make up the lost ground, as I had made a sort of objective in my mind of where I hoped to be within a certain time, therefore I calculated I still had 57km still to go, hoping to leave about 35 km for the next day, which meant now having to do 22 km in 3 hours before it got dark and cold. No matter I felt good. I was re-energized and settled down to enjoy the walk. I managed to find some good short cuts which must have saved a lot of time because I finally came to rest, just after another big climb at 3900 meters on the summit with a great view of the surrounding area, this left just 34km for tomorrow, to finally arrive in Shangri-La. It had been another perfect day and I had found another perfect place to set up camp.

It was a very cold night—12 inside the tent so consequently in the morning everything was frozen, my boots, my socks were solid which was like trying to put your foot inside a brick. Water had frozen inside my container which was inside my rucksack, so I could not warm any water and make my usual porridge like broth from oats that I was carrying with me, therefore having to skip breakfast and motivate myself to launch from out of my lovely warm sleeping bag out into the numbing cold. I quickly got packed away so that I could start walking and warm up.

The day felt hard again I think because of skipping breakfast and too much walking on tarmac which made it tiring and tedious with very little in the way of variety, just long twisting roads with thick forest on both sides. I had refused an invitation to eat a little earlier on when a little old man came running out and signalled me to come back with him, pointing towards his Tibetan farm house signalling me to rest and eat, but my mind was too focused on reaching Shangri-La today and felt that if I had stopped I might get too comfortable and tempted to get stuck there, looking back though I wished I had and started noticing how I seemed to be in such a rush, chasing something all the time, then when reaching there rushing off to the next idea. I felt I should be cherishing these incidental moments, giving them more time and exploring the magic of coincidental opportunities. I vowed to slow down a bit both my mind and my walking pace.

I plodded on more slowly this time pacing myself and peering at the endless horizon of hot tarmac ahead, time went slow and my legs felt like they were walking twice the distance until finally the last 4km they just stopped. I argued with them intensely and I think I heard them say "I don't care if it's only 4 more centimetres we are not moving" and so they promptly didn't.

Nothing to do, my legs had gone on strike and all I could do was find the nearest place to lie down. I rested for half an hour and whilst like that, with the weight of my legs I felt fine, until I tried getting up again and all I wanted to do then was be horizontal again. It was really hard to get going after that, I was strangely drained of any vertical ability. I forced myself to get up and keep going as it was not too far now and plodded onwards, finally after what felt like forever I arrived at around 5.30pm in another heavy, dirty, grey, dusty uninspiring place. My body did not care it had given up arguing some time back and had gone into `limp mode` slow but surely would get me home. I was hoping there was going to be a bit more to this place than what I was seeing; surely this was not the legendary Shangri La, as all I could see was grey concrete and dust blowing around, it has to represent the name somewhere, surely?

I needed to find a bank to change some money, if I had any hope of a room to sleep in tonight. I had been saving my last 20 Yuan for an emergency or a little luxury, and tonight I definitely wanted the luxury of a bad room that 20 Yuan might get me if I haggled a bit and looked desperate enough. I managed to find a bank but it had just closed, so it looked like option 2 of having to find that dingy room somewhere.

I was really tired now, hungry and hoped to come across something quick and easy as all I wanted to do now was to rest and take the weight off my shoulders. I stopped a friendly looking Chinese man, and with a few hand signs I tried to ask where a cheap room would be, he grinned from ear to ear put his hand on my shoulder like he had found an old friend.

"Ahhh I am an Indian my friend" He pronounced; this confused me straight away as he was obviously Chinese.

"also I am a Christian and I will take it on as my spiritual duty to find you a good cheap room" he beamed with a saintly glint in his eyes.

"Ok here we go, what am I getting myself into" I thought

After explaining he used to live in India but his home land was China and then explaining to him where, why, when, who I was, and that I was very tired and needed a cheap place to stay as I only had 20 Yuan left, he promptly marched me off around the corner to what looked like the 'dole office' in West Bromwich next to the re-rehabilitation centre for under aged single parent heroin addicts. He marched inside a narrow corridor then turned towards a serving hatch of some kind and rapped his knuckles hard on the remaining glass panel. A round stony faced woman appeared and a short sharp conversation ensued, which all sounded very aggressive as though he was demanding that she give me a room; the woman shook her head at first and looked at me with a blank discriminating look; OK I was a bit dirty I thought, unshaven and certainly did not smell too good, but looking around I was good enough for this place I was sure of it. In the end my Christian saviour, with holy conviction on his side suddenly raised the tempo a bit and waved his arms around throwing in a flurry of words that finally seemed to do the job and won the conflict; a slightly agitated woman seemingly to have `lost face` then silently led me up some grey concrete steps to my room; the approach to which was really grim and worsened the deeper we went inside; the whole ambience was depressing, grey, cold, broken and draughty. Someone coughed and it echoed the way echoes do in socially depressed high rise flats, lingering around slightly too long the way skid marks and tobacco stains do; it reverberated and bounced around the corridors, bumping into and arguing with toothless old men smelling of piss and yesterdays alcohol, a baby cried, someone threw up and a chill ran through my spine. I was too tired to be bothered about it and really I was ready to sleep anywhere, even here! shocked but amused with the extremity of it all I followed trying to imagine, or not to, what my room would be like. She led me to my room and it was half glazed as I expected and overlooked a busy junction outside where big trucks screeched to a halt simultaneously blazing their horns. I did have a TV though and an electric blanket that only one filament seemed to be working, so overall I was impressed! Maybe that was what the argument was about earlier and she was trying to charge extra for the luxuries!

Did I dare to use the toilets I thought to myself? I held back from that delight until later with the fear of serious skid marks building up I did have to dare to investigate. It was not hard to decide which direction they were and needed not to ask. I just knew it. I could feel their presence which I was sure was just around the next corner. First the acidic smell hit me then shortly followed by the classic drip, drip, dripping of faulty plumbing, then I saw them, a row of cubicles some with their doors dropped to one side, missing a hinge here and there in a depressing 'do not approach me attitude' and not shutting properly on purpose just to make the point of it all, resonating the fact that no one cares about me, only wants to use me. Cautiously and with the least contact of flesh possible, I pushed open one of the doors to a particularly depressed toilet, but within was proudly exposing its masterpiece of human waste and abuse; believe me there was no snow capped mountain here, but quite a few brown ones. I checked them all and in each cubicle there was a pyramid of human waste . . . . a brown mountain and a trickle of residue that was overflowing over the bowl and menacingly making its way creeping along the floor looking for something or someone to infest . . . . I ran away.

I went back to my room and felt disgusted, dirty, polluted. I could feel particles of that toilet area crawling all over me, in my nostrils, my skin, my mouth. I started to undress so as to feel a little bit cleaner but noticed that my various layers were equally a mess. I removed my boots and nearly threw up with the smell, my socks had been fermenting and were now highly toxic, sticky and took on an aggressive tone with me, hmmmmm! the hardships and perils of the road have taken their toll. I threw my socks in the corner of the room next to the door for protection against the living or the dead, amused at the idea for no one, nothing dead or alive would dare or be able to get past them. I chuckled to myself at the thought of 'guard socks' and started thinking that maybe I have neglected a little bit of personal hygiene over the last week or so; with that I heard one of the cubicles make a remark to that thought, it coughed, spat and then threw up a sticky brown lump resembling a statement which translated something like "get this anagram . . . . pot kettle the black calling." Yeah yeah I get it, and decided that the next priority for tomorrow after the bank must be to find a better place to stay and get on top of the hygiene situation and far away from this one.

I slept surprisingly well, maybe due to all the toxicity that were flying around in the air which must have rendered me unconscious and from which remarkably I did not contract any bad rashes or blood poisoning. With luck and health still on my side I got out of there as quickly as possible and then with a whole new day ahead of me I was free to explore, all day, no rush and take it easy.

I found the bank and changed some money and had that feeling of being financially cushioned again, so I headed out into the plethora of stalls, stands, shacks and shops that were buzzing with early morning activity, amused at all the people feeding and slurping of noodles, pots and dishes of this and that, which I never really got to grips with it all; I like to try most things and often did but I still did not know what I was eating most of the time, there were things being steamed, fried, boiled, rolled, grilled, flattened, chased, caught, killed, chopped and things that I am sure you were not supposed to eat and was just there for decoration.

I came upon a small local place to eat and sat down, immediately they came over and in full 'speed Chinese' babbled away to me and stood there waiting. Was I being insulted or invited to a wedding, not sure so I replied in English "I am hungry." Rubbed my stomach and pointed to all the Chinese characters painted in big red letters on the wall and shrugged my shoulders, thinking maybe this was either a prayer, song lyrics, or hopefully maybe a menu, but still they just froze there and did not seem to understand and still waiting for me to say something they could understand. I shrug then I see two others eating a big bowl of noodles full of vegetables and things . . . not sure quite what was floating but it looked good, so I point to them and say "I have that." Please. Shi shi.

After a good belly full of noodles and learning to 'slurp' properly I continued walking and soon realized that I must have entered in from a bad part of the town, because now the buildings started to become more modern, cleaner looking, less concrete and more colour splashed about, then up in front like an oriental oasis was an ancient village which rose up in a sea of quaint terracotta roof tops curled up at the edges where dragons spat fire in elemental battles; this was more like what I had expected. I was suddenly in the old original part within another maze of beautiful old traditional buildings, temples and guest houses. This was 'Shangrilla'. I selected a guest house or should I say it selected me; the one that was advertising 'hot water and showers available' and made sure I got my bearings and took a business card this time.

It was another Liajang and I was about to fall in love again with its charm, but this place was smaller giving it a really cute, homely, warm ambience. There were very few tourists so it was quiet and serene. I could imagine this place would be heaving normally, lots of places to stay to eat and shop, maybe I saw ten westerners all day. One of those was a French guy who was in the same dormitory as me. I spoke with him and exchanged stories; he had been travelling from Laos, hitch hiking with very little but carrying around a big accordion, he said it had proved to be a great way to interact and amuse people which got you attention and therefore got you information and got you places; in the evenings it broke through all the language barriers and everyone would smile, clap and join in understanding a universal common language of music.

It turned out that we were both heading to Dequin which was 200 km away to the north and the last outpost before the forbidden land . . . . Tibet. I explained I wanted to try and get a bus ride from Dequin to Lhasa and I was hoping he might have some advice, tricks and ideas for that, but apart from a magic accordion and being able to play a neat little French tune and do a little dance, he had no advice. I liked his attitude though and we talked some more then planned to try to hitch hike to Dequin together tomorrow.

I had a good long talk with my new friend about travelling and life in general, and came to the same conclusion with him; that each time it gets harder and harder to return to the west and have indeed substituted one vice for another, this addiction to has led me to many strange places and to talk with many strange faces, initially starting off being filled with so many ideals, romanticism, judgements, which very quickly through experiences get dissolved to the point of not knowing what is normal any more. It is all normal in the end. We are only what we believe we are, what we have been told, labelled and educated. There is no 'normal' but by experiencing as much diversity as possible we find more pieces to the puzzle and start to see a huge labyrinth of diversity, but we, the I, the ego that has formed an image about itself, decided how it wishes to appear to others and the world, and defends this image so violently at times; is just a fragmentation of a greater and more complete and truthful personality. We are like the leaves on a great huge tree looking at all the other leaves around us, some young, some old, some green, some yellow, bigger or smaller, making distinctions between us, yet if we look deep and far we see the twig, the branch, the tree trunk, the root and finally the seed and even the spark of life that created it. Finally if you go far enough you see we are exactly the same, and that we all carry the blue print within us, and a piece of the final message or picture, each culture, each person, each point of view is a unique mirror to our true identity, we can only truly know ourselves through the eyes of others.

Every time that I returned back home I took home with me much more souvenirs than what I did not buy; that was a new pair of eyes, new vision and seemed to be seeing with their eyes. I saw more and more that was wrong; having too much of everything subsequently becoming complacent and bored, distracted with various entertainments and gadgets, we seemed to own so much stuff which in the end became to own us, as our minds became preoccupied with it all, full of fear and paranoia, worried about it if breaks, or is stolen, or becomes out of date, unfashionable, this was not freedom and happiness that it all advertised and promised. Finally I saw how lost so many people looked, aggressive, defensive, fearful and unhappy, reflecting the increasing reports of social, physical and mental health problems, with all our resources and choices that are available to us, we should be in perfect condition and healthy. We are missing something, lost something, some experience maybe. I meet with eyes of many people here, often very poor, desperate, struggling, hungry, but they still have life in their eyes, they have lived small lives but fully, they have truly loved in their lives, they have truly surrendered to something much bigger and more truthful. They know what it is, how simple and pure it is and that you do not need to travel thousands of miles to find it, it was always right here. They still have time for you, are not consumed with fear and therefore welcome you into their homes, for the simple beauty of wanting to know and learn about someone different to themselves, and still remembering how to smile, because they never forgot.

The eyes I was starting to see back home were cold, grey and discriminating, too busy, too much clutter, too much stress, technology was supposed to make things easier more efficient, it didn't it just accelerated everything so that we buy twice as much, work twice as hard to pay for things that cost twice as much. Two jobs, two cars, two wives, too much. Enough . . . . we blow our minds out in the bars and clubs to forget, to hope for real love, that comes every weekend packed inside a pill, the modern paradigm to treat the symptom not the cause. We buy our love and hope to pay the ferry man when that dark day cashes in on our soul.

Yet they are playing catch up also here; they see us tourists, they see our gadgets and fancy clothes and we are walking wallets to them, they become to want the things we have, but do not realize they are dancing in the shadows of our mistakes, and will become like us and realize that there is always a price to pay for the things that we want, and often that costs us our smiles.

Only man tries to destroy memories in the fires of his deceit, but those men will never burn the shadows that remain in the ashes of history, though they will try.

In a fuel injected engine there is an electronic flow meter, it measures air flow. It is a tube that sits in line of the air intake system and has a fine wire running through the middle, called a hot wire system, because an electric current is passed through the wire which creates a certain temperature just like the element in an electric fire. Air flows over the wire as the car accelerates and cools it down, the cooler the wire becomes, more electricity is then needed to heat up the wire to get it back to its base temperature, the difference in current needed to achieve this can then be used to calculate the amount of air that is flowing down into the engine so that the correct amount of fuel can be injected and maintain perfect air fuel ratio, all this is controlled by the black box, the cars brain, a computer, but the principle of balance that I am trying to describe is the same. Everything is energy, the stuff around us and even our thoughts. The more you use the more you have to put back and visa versa, this principle of balance is the pendulum that has been swinging from one extreme to the other through out our lives, we live and experience this constant movement of the pendulum clinging on to it for dear life like a roller coaster ride. Life is constant movement; I wondered what it must be like to let it go of it. To stop clinging!

Like motor mechanics if the engine is out of balance it will not function well and eventually break, the harder you push it the hotter it gets and therefore more fuel it consumes. Maybe some of us would benefit from a bit of re-wiring, or an experience, so that we are able to understand what we are doing when we put our pedal down to the floor.

The next morning I was eager to get going again, wanting to stamp down hard on that accelerator pedal, not feeling fully relaxed and thinking too hard about the next part of the puzzle which would be trying to get into Tibet; the uncertainty was hanging around like a storm cloud that was getting closer, darker and wondering if it was going to pass you by without getting a thrashing. My impatience was tested further with the relaxed attitude of the French company I was in . . . . taking far too long with a 'petite dejuener' which prompted a late start and finally set off together down a dusty hot road just after midday, therefore my enthusiasm had been a bit deflated as I felt that it was a bit late now to be starting off, fighting with myself again this element of 'time' and always feeling the need to be chasing it. I looked at my friends relaxed care free attitude, a mirror to myself, which was showing me what I was not at this time.

At first we had many vans stop but they all turned out to be taxi touts trying to get some business in and soon sped off again realizing we were trying to hitch a ride for free. Then an old couple stopped and sped off when we tried to get in, maybe they recognized the French guy who must have terrorized them before with his accordion! eventually a big 4by4 with an even bigger Chinese guy stopped and after a bit of confusing dialogue in different languages I think we managed to explain where we wanted to go and hoped that he had agreed to take us as far as he could. Looking confused but in a 'compelled to help us out sort of a way' he impatiently signalled us to get in as though he was in a rush. It was a great big comfy ride, but soon he kept trying to ask us something and we kept telling him "Dequin" and pointing straight ahead, he seemed to be getting frustrated and nervous, and I got the impression he was trying to say that it was a long way, which we knew and then he did the money thing with his fingers. I shrugged and replied, "mee ho" no have. He carried on driving but I could feel tension starting to build up, he got a call on his cell and seemed a little more agitated afterwards and again he turned to us and tried to ask something. I was sure he was expecting us to pay and started to get more agitated. Finally I signalled to stop and with a walking motion of my fingers he promptly stopped and let us out. We had managed to travel quite far already and now the scenery had changed dramatically, all around there was a panoramic backdrop of towering mountains, which were the Himalayas, for the first time I really saw them, immense and instantly I felt so small. The road we were on was following a river that was cutting a deep crevasse through solid rock. I tried to follow the road ahead with my eyes as far as I could see, but it stretched for miles and miles. It was the craziest road I have ever seen just snaking upwards in an endless maze of switchbacks, climbing through impossible elevated landscape trying to make its way northwards daring to penetrate the depths of the Himalayas.

We both stood there admiring the view and then just as I was about to pick up my backpack resigning ourselves to walk for a while, another car came to a halt without us even trying and looked like he was stopping to give us a lift, this was incredible what perfect timing.

"Nee how, chee chu Dequin." Hello I go Dequin.

"Yes" He replied in velly good Ingrish, nodding and smiling frantically. He was a middle aged Chinese man and very friendly and relaxed this time, and very happy to take us all the way to Dequin where he lived; it looked like everything was going to work out perfectly in the end and I was amazed to think we would get to Dequin after such a late start to the day. The road was incredible as it became more and more elevated, hours and hours of endless switch backs over huge mountain passes, high altitude temples and sporadic dwellings that were lost in antiquity and frozen in an ancient time zone.

When we arrived in Dequin it was already late in the evening and dark, and we were all very hungry so I suggested we should find a place to eat and offer to buy good meal for our driver. We found a place and ate together in a sort of embarrassed silence of noodle slurping, then afterwards to break the silence we made good friends with the owners by the way of the magic accordion, out it came and my friend went straight into his routine, the transformation was instant and a universal language now flowed and connected us all; clapping and dancing we became for an instance one mind. Very soon our minds fragmented again and one of them produced a bottle of Chinese wine.

" It velly good." They said, but I would have used the word `wine` and especially 'very' extremely loosely that described a red liquid that should be applied and never drunk. After applying the medicine internally and politely nodding with approval, the magic accordion finally said farewell.

The next morning I talked with my French companion about what his plans were, thinking if he had come all this way just to turn back again, so I offered for him to join me on my quest to Lhasa; of which the uncertainty and sketchiness of it all certainly seemed to tempt him. We discussed my plans a little further of which I could not really expand any further, then came up with an idea and seemed to have convinced him it would be a good to climb the mountain just up ahead, explaining that from up there I was sure there would be a really good view, and . . . . I hesitated at that point as I found myself bit lost for any other explanation, and then as though I had just found my script again, continued to explain enthusiastically that once we get up there I would know where to go and maybe we could drop down on to a road the other side that I hoped and imagined would be there, from where we could start hitching. After a short pause he agreed!

"wow he really is crazy!" I thought.

Hungry for adventure we both set off immediately towards the mountain, took a side road, then a track, then a trail that seemed to be going in the right direction. The trail soon became steep and water that had been running down from above had formed huge areas of ice as smooth as glass, with no way to go around we gingerly attempted to cross over it, but it soon became clear that my friend was in no way prepared to follow where I was prepared or stupid enough to go, his old worn out Doc.Martins boots were totally smooth and had no grip at all, his jacket was very thin and was he was already complaining about the cold, his hands were numb; basically he had no equipment with him at all except a very amusing accordion . . . . ! I could hear him sliding around behind me down below, slipping and cursing, clutching of and snapping of branches . . . .

"putain du merd." I heard him curse again. This time I reached down to pass him one of my walking poles, but his gangly legs were busy skating and dancing all over like a frantic giraffe, after I had stopped laughing I took on a more serious tone and in the end I told him I admired his determination and spirit but better to turn back before something serious happens like breaking his accordion!

We parted company soon after that, obvious that we were on different types of adventures. We said farewell and wished each other well on our travels.

Later that day, just for my curiosity, I went to the bus station to see if I could get a bus ticket to Lhasa. I went up to the ticket counter trying to appear as confident as possible and asked

"Nee chee Lhasa shee shee." I go Lhasa thank you . . . . grinning wildly and waving a handful of Yuan.

"Mee ho." . . . . No! Came back a stern reply. Seemed that no bargaining was to be done here at all, just a straight no. I asked for a few closer destinations hoping to get just inside the border of Tibet, but the same reply came back, no, no and definitely no! You are a foreigner and we cannot sell you a ticket it is not allowed, it is forbidden!

With that I started to think about the option of hitching to one of the next towns just inside of Tibet and then maybe it would be easier from there to get a bus ride once that I am already in. Either way I was not about to give up and had come too far not to try, anything!

I started off heading out of town but it was getting a bit late now to be hitching, then thought about our last success and decided to give it a go. The road was terrible, and full of big trucks carrying rock and earth, kicking up plumes of dry dust from the unfinished road, sun was in my eyes and it all started to feel a bit oppressive. I managed to find a quiet place in my mind and then settled down into a steady walk. A white van stopped and my spirits lifted, as though the universe had felt my point of no return in my mood and decided to help me with getting a little further away from these trucks. As it came to a halt I immediately noticed it was completely crammed full with Chinese and they were all pretty girls, elevating my mood even further. I opened the door to much giggling and smiling, some of them could speak a little English so I told them I wanted to go to Lhasa, which they all returned looks of disbelief, they said they were sorry but only going as far as the temple, which was just 12km away, but every bit helps I thought so I got in; besides no way was I going to miss the chance of shoe horning myself in between this lot. Maybe it was some sort of a dream, maybe I should refuse, maybe it is a cunning trap.

I shrugged my shoulders, removed my back and squeezed myself into places where I had dreamed to, should not do, and were not possible to, but for the next desperately too few miles we chatted, giggled and I sighed, waiting to wake up, but after some more cute giggling and exchanging stories they invited me to join them on a little trekking they were planning to do, around some local mountain villages and sight seeing. Suddenly it was very easy to forget about my own personal plans and I was already gone . . . . take me to your leader I am all yours.

The next day we set off together and walked along beautiful trails following a deep gorge up into forest and beyond to into remote mountain villages, Tibetan and Chinese culture lost in time beneath snow covered peaks and glaciers cascading down into deep valleys. I very quickly forgot about Lhasa, hitch hiking and time, to be honest it just did not seem to exist here or even matter. I was really enjoying this unplanned opportunity, just enjoyed the here and now of it all, the simplicity and timelessness that permeated all around this area. It seemed very normal to be able to just call in any one of the Tibetan homes that we frequently came upon; the girls would knock on one of their door and ask if was possible to come in and that we needed something to eat and drink, they all welcomed us in happily and provided whatever they could. Their homes were simple and sparse but always our hosts were very happy to welcome you in and offered us what ever they could, they appeared to have very little in the way of luxuries; looking around I saw that life here was obviously hard, but they were very helpful, peaceful and friendly. They ate very simple food which did not vary much from Tibetan bread, soup, and always a big pot of green tea. I was very quickly humbled by these people, I watched them the way they moved it was like they glided to where they wanted to be making sure they did not make and harsh movements or sounds, the way they placed things in front of us, so gently, the way they all conducted themselves. Life was like a sacred ritual, every part of it every detail had divine significance. Their simple homes were a living working temple and the people and guests were divine beings. I concentrated on the exchange of words between each other which were so quietly spoken, with what I perceived to be the utmost sincerity, concentration, respect and peacefulness in the tone of their voices. I told this to one of the girls about these sensations I was getting, whether I had been receptive and correct with my presumptions, she could speak a little English and told me that my perceptions had been very accurate, that the conversations they were having between these people and themselves were some of the most beautiful exchanges of human contact you could imagine, to the point of being poetic. I suddenly remembered an earlier conversation I had with a Chinese guy, who I had been explaining to him how beautiful I thought the Chinese characters looked to me and I was fascinated by their construction and meanings after having some of them explained, and how they were evolved from an ancient language of pictogram s, which when used in various places and positions with others it was possible to create endless ways of expressing things, he said that I could not possibly imagine the depth and beauty of Chinese language, even for a native speaker it is impossibly to reach its limitations of expression.

I started thinking about my own country and imagined doing this, walking into someone's property and asking if we can come in and eat and talk philosophy, they would look at us very strange and probably have us arrested or shoot us . . . . !

The evening was starting to close in and we talked about finding a suitable place to ask if we could stay the night, after all agreeing it would be a good idea we continued walking and very soon came across an old Tibetan farmhouse, again very basic with a few animals, mules, chickens, goats. We knocked on the door and it was answered by a very lively bubbly young Tibetan woman, who came out to greet us, smiling from ear to ear. After a short conversation it became clear that she was very happy to have us as guests. She wasted no time and quickly showed us to a large room where we could sleep in; actually it was a corner of their barn with a few beds and things that they stored there, but the beds were plenty and blankets were thick. It had a very particular atmosphere and felt so peaceful, quiet, protected with a stillness that I think was accentuated by the sheer mass of the building having walls of huge stone and mud over a meter thick. It felt safe warm and quiet, with an atmosphere that I can only describe as like a nativity scene if you could imagine that of, fresh hay, beeswax, candle light and incense it was just like that, beautifully simple, uncomplicated. I felt that I could completely relax that any troubles were insignificant and my true self shone out from within. I was truly at peace. Again there was no passing of time to be aware of, or memories; my home, the west where I was born were just some residue memory like a dream. I had a feeling that nothing existed outside of these walls unless I actually thought about it and went out there to look for it again. I felt released from all responsibility, it did not exist it was just an illusion of memory, and that made me appreciate and see more that was happening around me in this moment, this was the only true reality the only thing to be sure of, here and now!

The bubbly young woman was called Chorma, and was also the name to a beautiful Tibetan song that I heard last week whilst staying at the Tibetian geust house of which that evening of wibbly wobbly dancing and song, whereby they had specifically played this one song entitled `Chorma` a haunting enchanting melody and I must admit made the hairs on the back of my neck stand up. A tear welled up as I remembered and my heart warmed. Chorma was a good name for our host remembering how beautiful this song was which reflected her beauty and spirit. I could imagine her parents had chosen her name after listening to such a song. She was not particularly physically beautiful, she had the same sort of hard leathery appearance that this high altitude climate produces, but she was certainly radiant, with a contagious smile. There were no issues here or complicated clutter in her mind or in her heart, just completely happy with what, who, why, and when. Not wanting, not seeking, not needing, just being. I felt quickly frustrated not being able to communicate with her wanting to know more about her life, thoughts and ideas about her world and what she thought of ours, but all I could do was continue to watch and admire from the depths of my imagination, from which I found myself deep within a movie that was forming and a telepathic conversation with her, we became spiritually bonded far exceeding the boundaries of spoken language, we got married, I settled in Tibet with our expanding family . . . . and I was gone . . . . I really wanted to marry her; live the life of this movie, my mind jumped on a roller coaster ride of bliss saturated fantasy almost to the point of no return, when a safety valve suddenly blew and like an inverted bungee jump I was back in the room . . . . music crackled out from some impossible plastic antique which prompted the start to the obligatory dancing to Tibetan music, which seemed to be their passion and their way of entertainment. Later on I taught them how to play some card games, simple ones at first which they soon became experts and demanded for more. I introduced more complex and competitive rules, Chorma giggled and laughed all night long, all of them very easily adapting and keeping up with the level of complexity, it was as if they never doubted that they would not be able to understand or learn, it was almost exhausting to watch her relentless happiness and enthusiasm, not caring who won or lost but amused by it all and learning new things, the moment and the pleasure of being with others.

A conversation developed about what we were going to do over the next few days and the idea came up that it would be good to stay here for Christmas . . . . Wow! was it Christmas eve already? I had lost all track of time and had not thought about these things much, as the last few years of travelling I had become to reflect too much on this time of the year and the contrasts became too great and I needed to be away from it all, but this time I was very happy at the thought of being together with these people in such a simple environment. I talked with my friends and we thought it would be a good idea if some of us (the hunter gatherers, the men) went to the nearest market and bought some fresh supplies back here to cook a good Christmas meal for everyone, as they seemed to be in short supply and maybe we could get a few luxuries.

We came to learn that Chorma's parents had gone away leaving her and her brother to run their small holding. We discovered her parents had gone on a very important pilgrimage to Llahsa where they would be devoting many days of prayer and worship. I got the impression that it was either a once in a lifetime thing or to bless an up an coming family marriage, either way I could sense that it was a great deal for them all. After some discussion with Chorma, who did not need much convincing, she beamed with approval at the idea of celebrating Christmas together but said that the nearest market was a 6 hour walk and a 2 hour taxi ride. We all agreed this was not a problem so she fetched her mobile phone; it was decorated and dangling with all sorts of terrible plastic Chinese cartoon effigies which seemed to be obligatory and necessary to make Asian telephone calls.

I watched her make the call and one of the pink plastic chickens started flashing. I was almost impressed enough to want one for my own phone. I was wondering if their phones worked the same as ours in the west, because here they seemed to need to remove it from their ear then shout at it from the top of their voices, but it seemed to work for them and she had soon arranged for a taxi to meet us on the nearest accessible part of the road.

The next morning greeted us again with clear deep blue skies and a wintry blast of cold air. The light was intense, crisp definition casting long frosty shadows, but our icy breath was soon warmed up with cups of steaming Tibetan tea, bread and a fiery chilly relish to dip it in. We huddled Around a smoky clay built cooker, that was struggling to stay alight for some reason, whereby faces peered at each other through a smoky haze, not any of us wanting to really make much of conversation just waiting for some warmth either from the tea, the fire or the chilli paste that would give us some enthusiasm to organize ourselves for the long day ahead.

The chilli paste ran out first, being that it seemed to be the one thing that worked really well that got you moving around, involuntary hopping about and fanning your mouth. Then with fiery breath and an internal coating of the finest Tibetan tea we finally got going and set off back the way we had came; ascending a steep valley which had us very quickly warm and sweating. It was a long walk back up the side of the valley from the lower altitude of the river, where Chormas village was, and then a long dusty taxi ride into town from there. We tried to find as many interesting things as possible from a very uninteresting store; even they seemed to have very little, just a few fresh vegetables were the luxuries here, so we took what we could and set off to make the journey back. We struggled to find a taxi driver who was prepared to take us down a rough dirt road to where we could walk back from, they all knew this road and that is was in a bad way, steep with huge pot holes and boulders strewn all over from rock falls above it. After some bartering we eventually found one who agreed he would take us, but I became suspicious when a little later he stopped to wash his car! I don't think he really knew what this road was going to be like, he has just washed his car, so no way is he going to take us down that track we came up when he sees it. Sure enough we turned off from the main road and started to descend down a very narrow steep track, he kept hesitating, stopping and starting whilst continually muttering, then got out and removed a few rocks from ahead seemingly to make a big scene out of it, stalling and obviously trying to make excuses now to get out of his agreed contract with us. This continued for another 20 minutes until he eventually stopped and told us he was not going any further. I was a little agitated as was my friend because this meant an extra 2 hours walk down a steep mountainous valley with many bags of shopping, he knew where we wanted to go at the beginning and had agreed. Now he wanted to ditch us where we were and he still wanted paying. It was also getting late now with little time left to argue, the sun was now already very low in the sky and losing light. My Chinese friend started to argue with the driver which reached an intense pitch, then came to a sudden stand off; both must have said some serious words and were both now desperately trying not to lose face, there was an air of ancient Asian pride at stake, you could feel it like electricity in the air and I half suspected at any moment now that the lip sink would suddenly slip a time frame behind and the whole scene would erupt into a full on Bruce Lee scene, with 'Shaolin' power fists and energy bolts of dragon breath. I tried to insist to just forget it we did not have any extended play here and the way the taxi drivers eyes were glowing green with fireballs for fists; I thought it better to lose face and get going.

With the fading light against us we did lose face and having to pay him but we insisted he show us a short cut that he spoke about, pointing directly down, and eventually we got him to show us where it started from. We followed him through someone's house then out into the back yard to find a steep trail, my friends made him walk all the way down carrying some of our bags for us, still not being sure if this short cut was indeed short, but finally arrived at where we were picked up in the morning, we had lost a lot of time by now, the sun had already disappeared and we strode on as fast as we could but I knew it was just a matter of time before it would be completely dark with no torch and no moon at this time either. I estimated to be exactly where we did not want to be in full dark trying to descend the perilous valley track that snaked its way down to the valley below, of which the path was often only just wide enough for a small Chinese foot, next to that was a near vertical cliff, that plummeted down to the raging river far below. We raced on trying not to think about the 'what ifs' with sweat breaking out into monsoon season, streaking tributaries ran down from my forehead, half walking, half running with no magic reindeer to carry our Xmas booty, we were two Santa's dragging our plastic bags of vegetables which majestically bounced around threatening to break and put these two Santa's in a very un-festive mood. We both were silent, lost in doubt as we both knew it would not be good stumbling about on the side of this ravine in the dark, knowing how bad this trail was, very narrow and at times that had us hard up against the rock face edging along where parts of the path had eroded and fallen, there was no room for error and nothing to hold on to, no reset button or extra life left, just a long way down to the raging river below. This was just a normal days walk for the locals here, their main highway so to speak, who we often saw herding their goats and yaks along. We hurried along as fast as possible, but darkness slowly and surely engulfed us. Not being able to see well we were reduced to creeping along very carefully as this part of the trail split and took many turns. The shadows of the night played tricks of the mind which questioned us regularly as to where we were, was this the way? How far was the bridge that we used this morning which crossed over the river? Had we missed it? Had we walked too far and took a wrong turn already? no way to see ahead there was nothing for reference, no house lights, nothing, just blackness and a vague impression of light coloured ground beneath our feet where the path was. Hours must have passed wasting time losing the path, having to double back, tired, hungry and quickly losing track of time and distance.

I stopped fighting, knowing that we had already lost the race and stared up into the heavens for inspiration, instantly trillions of stars bathed me in wonder and for a moment I was hypnotized and lost amongst them, I felt so peaceful. I was not lost. I was not concerned. I had a feeling again of being exactly where I should be, that it was correct, that the only thing to fight was fear, doubt and to not rush, not to make a mistake and everything would be good.

My friend behind me was struggling and I could hear his nervousness, tiredness, bad placement of feet. I could hear him stumbling and muttering, struggling not being able to see. I reassured him to take it easy, to slow down as much as we needed to be safe. It was dark now anyway so no point in rushing. I realized then I was carrying my camera which has a small light and comes on for a few seconds to assist the auto focus mechanism. I thought it would maybe just be enough to briefly see where the path was. It was better than nothing at all and with this we were able to continue following snippets of the trail like parts of a video tape that had been erased making up the bits in between with our imagination, and pupils dilating and re adjusted in between the sporadic lighting. Slowly we descended down the steep trail. Then with much relief it started to flatten out and finally fully opened out onto the valley floor, whereby we could not find the trail it just sort of dissolved into hundreds of crossing animal tracks, so with nothing to orientate us inevitable despair seemed to be waiting for us. I imagined us stumbling around like this until dawn in freezing conditions. Neither of us had anything to offer in the way of enthusiasm, or ideas, and our instincts were being diplomatic and stood down, the only option was to take a wild guess and keep moving. Gloomily we both plodded on until we stopped and noticed a light some way ahead off to our right over the other side of the river, it looked like someone was waving a torch, or maybe it was a star it did not matter either way we were going to follow it. I signalled back with my camera and a succession of rapid movements came back confirming someone was out there. Sometimes good things do not come easy and today had been one of those days.

A little bit further we found the bridge where we had crossed earlier this morning and soon after crossing we were all reunited again and much relieved, tired, very hungry and cold. Chorma had started to get concerned with our late arrival and had come out to be a human beacon. I was wet all over with sweat and calculated it had taken us 14 hours to get back but the thought of that farmhouse and familiar friendly faces soon energized me again. I looked forward to be re united with the others and back at the nativity scene to celebrate the festivities together. Her light in the end had guided us in the right direction which led us over the rope bridge to the village on the other side. The village of mud houses, their flat roofs, simple and functional, they did look like something from Bethlehem with a slight Chinese twist for there was no room at the inn and had decided to go for a walk, but did arrive at the stables following a bright star, where there was a newly born goat, Chinese incense, and a few slightly wiser men (and women).

Chorma was literally jumping with joy when she saw our modest gift of vegetables, we certainly did feel like Santa Clause that day and immediately set about distributing them so that we could all help her to chop and prepare a Christmas dinner. Very soon a huge wok was steaming over a blazing fire, precious little plastic pots were hunted down and located from the depths of `special occasion` recesses, and soon she had an exotic palette of strange powders, and spices. Instinctively she began adding a pinch of this, then a shake of that, concentrating on the large wok watching the signs, the steam, the bubbles, the spitting oil, intercepting at the right moment with a precision of Alchemical timing. This was nothing to do with cooking, this was Tibetan witchcraft. Steam mixed with exotic spices rose up in a spectacular display, ghostly tendrils stretched out from within the wok, twisting, dancing weaving mystery and magic into the air. The fabric of the cosmos seemed to reveal itself momentarily as glowing faces peered through its cracks. We all huddled around the wok and watched intensely this shadow pantomime, which was well under way and the spell hypnotizing us all. I watched as a fiery phoenix rose up to dance with dragons of the four corners of the earth, consumed itself, then died again to rise up once more, whilst the mill of the universe looked down upon us continuing to turn and grind indefinitely within the infinity of the moment.

Finally the ingredients had been purified and transformed enough, the great work was achieved, soup, rice and an exotic transformation of vegetables had been set out on a low wooden table, then Chormas brother suddenly stood up with a glint of mischief in his eyes, rushed off to another dark corner of the room to return with a plastic bottle of clear liquid . . . . my mind recoiled slightly, knowing what might be coming and started thinking of polite excuses, but he obviously wanted to make the most of this evening and excitedly debated with Chorma, there seemed to be some sort of discussion as to whether it would be permitted either from their parents or some other deeper restriction. Finally Chorma nodded as though she had gone through in her mind all the family and spiritual repercussions coming to the conclusion that karma would still be intact and was not going to hinder any unfavourable reincarnations later on, so with that we distributed the liquid between us leaving just enough for their parents, toasted to each other and down it went, in turn we all winced and screwed up our faces in response to that familiar stage one ignition burn, followed by the atomic detonation in the depths of your being. We ate a great meal, mixed with hot Chilli paste and Tibetian bread followed by dancing. We laughed all night letting time slip away as did each of our various stories and lives, slowly dissolving and becoming far away memories.

I was really enjoying the human contact of it all and was already thinking about having to leave them soon, fighting with thoughts of what I were doing just a few days before, reminding myself that I had been on a particularly solitary mission, this had felt like a holiday away from personal desires, goals, and ambitions living in the moment was irresponsibly easy sometimes. I felt that I was very much here and now and I was more than happy to wonder around these valleys, mountains and villages for the rest of my time . . . . but just one thing kept nagging at me, so many people said I would not be able to get to Lahsa that you will not make it, made me want to do it even more, the trap of the ego. I pulled back from the here and now and returned to the forbidden road, my mind suddenly waved goodbye to China and Chorma and decided that here and now will have to be another place to have to return to someday.

In the morning I was solemn this part was coming to an end and my attention was on the sky. I had taken it for granted because for weeks now it had been cloudless, not having to think of bad weather as it was consistently blue, but now each day had seen more and more big cumulus boiling up far in the distance towards the north. I realized I had become slightly complacent and got used to walking under clear blue skies, but winter storms must around somewhere and surely be well overdue, there was no news that snow had fallen anywhere yet and I started thinking that I really must get going whilst things are so favourable.

The Forbidden Road

Chapter 8

I sit here frozen like a startled rabbit, numb still from the events of the last 24 hours. I am covered in dust, mud, grime, snot . . . . and freezing to the core of my being, somewhere behind that glazed expression is me.

I am dazed.
I am amazed.
I am shocked . . .

. . . . but very much alive!

I recall the events just one day before replaying various bits of it in my minds eye; the marathon road trip that lay just a few seconds ahead of my unknowing as I set off down an uncertain road, a forbidden road, with the only certainty of being uncertain, and hoped a ride would come along soon.

That morning I had felt unusually good and positive; there was love welling up in my heart and I felt as clear as the blue sky above me, just as cloudless and unhindered by doubt. The distance ahead of me did not matter I was sure something would happen and that I will get through here. The feeling was overwhelming and I had to stop just to feel it, to respect it, to allow it recognition. I gazed peacefully around me becoming transfixed in the distance, where a huge horizon of white tipped mountains pierced the heavens. They regarded them here as sacred mountains and in that moment I could understand why. I felt them as though they were watching me, their power, and their wisdom. They looked so beautiful, so close and again I felt as though I could reach out and touch them. I could have stayed in this place indefinitely, my mind, my heart so completely surrendered. I felt a kind of death, but it was beautiful, no fear just surrender and then being cradled by it. My mind was so still in timelessness there was no need for anything, no desire, no fight just an incredible feeling of deep love, respect, honour and of letting go, of faith . . . . I let it all go and I turned away to follow a road I did not care where, when or how I just knew this was the way I was to go and everything was going to be fine.

Very few cars passed me, just the occasional truck with its cloud of dust chasing after it, taxi cabs, and two domestic cars who just waved something back at my hopeful gestures of getting a ride, they sounded their horns and sped on by! but what was I expecting the prospect of someone just stopping so early on in the morning and taking me all the way to Lhasa which was 1,700km from here and somehow getting through all the check points, something that I refused to try to think about . . . . questions, then a sudden snow shower of doubt swept over me and I suddenly felt cold and alone as I looked back at the long, dusty, desolate road behind me and still no cars in sight. I sighed and shook the cobwebs of doubt from my mind, put some sunshine back into my stride and started to just enjoy the morning again the here and now of it all. I slowed my pace down and told myself that its just a matter of time, everything happens when it is ready to, so many infinite possibilities that are just outside of my radar, I know they are coming and I must be open to receive them, so able, so free, how beautiful this feeling was. I had everything I needed, tent, food, cooker, what else did I need?

Suddenly a big black 4by4 materialized like a D'Lorean from out of the future, closely followed by a cloud of choking dust, maybe this was the devil come to trade my soul for a bus ticket ride to hell? I had not been listening to the road behind me and it caught me by surprise. I turned quick and stuck out my hand, it reacted and stopped immediately, my spirits raised with the first successful ride and so early on in the morning. The window went down and a friendly face appeared.

"Nee chee Markham." I asked . . . I go Markham, this was the first place marked on my map just within the border of Tibet and where I hoped I could try to buy a bus ticket. He seemed not to understand where I wanted to go so then I pointed up the road and said Lhasa, he shook his head but pointed up the road and gestured for me to get in. I was grateful for the ride regardless how far it was going as long as it was in the right direction not that there was much choice in these parts apart from up or down, everywhere else was pretty much un-navigable the terrain was unbelievable rugged, elevated and even this road which was a major highway was full of craters with various rock falls, but luckily the big 4by4 took it all in its stride and sped along eating up the kilometres. A few times he tried to communicate something but all it sounded like to me was a barrage of aggressive sounds which sounded like he was very concerned and frustrated about something. I tried not to get paranoid so all I could do was smile and say a few random words that I had picked up which seemed to break the ice but did not really reveal anything for either of us.

I clocked the trip meter and at the last count got to 75km, shortly after that he stopped and seemed to be saying that he needed to eat.

"how cha." Very good I say and I rubbed my stomach saying that I am also hungry then he waved me goodbye and went inside what looked to be a port a-cabin presumably to eat and waved me goodbye . . . . that was the end of that then I guessed and maybe he was not satisfied with the conversation we was not having.

I set off walking again down the road which had now become even more dusty, dry and very hot as the sun intensified. I was in the bottom of a deep valley what looked like an open cast coal mine and the way ahead was twisting, climbing, crazy labyrinth of road, rock, river all struggling with each other to decide who should dominate the other like a game of scissors, paper, stone . . . . this time the road was winning as it carved itself through rock and span the gaps of rivers to disappear in a shimmering haze of heat and dust.

Well I was 70 km closer to Lhasa! and it was still morning. I walked for maybe another 2 hours passing by some small villages, curious faces following my progress amused by my presence. I wave, smile and say: "Tashi delek" A Tibetan greeting that means something like, 'I hope you are blessed in every way and good fortune go with you for the rest of your day' or that's what I would like to think it meant as they seem very pleased when you address them this way.

Still walking but no cars, where are they all? I was starting to feel a little isolated and daunted by the terrain and the huge distance ahead . . . !

Then I hear engines in the distance behind me, I turn to look and see a big cloud of dust and maybe at least 5 cars. I really wanted one of them to stop, so when they got close enough I practically stepped out in front of them and tried to wave them down not wanting to miss any opportunity and really wanting to get some ground covered . . . . 1, 2, 3 of the cars all sped past, engulfing me in a choking cloud of dust. I see the last car now but I think he is already about to drive past. I put my hand out in a vain attempt to catch this last ride. I think and sense he is going to go past and start to feel disappointment set in, but suddenly he brakes hard and comes sliding to a halt next to me, it took me by surprise and I excitedly run up to the window. I ask for the next place on my map thinking it better to not mention Lhasa. "Markham" I say hopefully, immediately he nodded and I feel great, blessed by the universe again. I open the door and get into a good 4by4 with what looks to be 'Frank Zappa' at the wheel from Tibet and my mood is elevated with amusement and confidence, a little at a time, I think to myself and slowly but surely we will get there not be too greedy.

I settle down to enjoy the ride and think back to a few hours ago, early this morning walking into uncertainty and thinking about these travel Gods who often seem to assist in times of need and uncertainty for the love of travel, the adventure, the variety, the highs and lows that give me moments of clarity and insights, when the waters become calm and crystal clear, the sights, sounds and sensations that stimulate the soul and somehow answer ancient questions that elude me in my daily routines of life, or maybe remind me of previous incarnations, karma, slowly and silently they bubble to the surface, my doubts get answered as I travel, dancing with the elements of this planet both human and that which is not. The pieces of the puzzle click into place one by one as I advance the agenda to somewhere, feeling more whole, more complete, behind me my footprints that leave a legacy of ripples in the fabric of time.

The Gods answer me as they always do, but only when I am humble and ask for the right things nothing more or less than what I need is all I asked for this time. There is normally always a catch though, something I did not think about realising I was not specific enough. I wanted a ride, I wanted to get to Lhasa, I did not say how I wanted to get there. I did not care . . . . !

I remember thinking this morning, I wonder where I will be tonight? I reflected on this thought some time later as I pushed his head away from the gear lever where he had left it after passing out. He groaned as I pushed him away, then struggled with the gear lever that did not seem to be attached to the gearbox, so that I could get this bloody vehicle out of here, before it either falls apart, or we all freeze to death on the spot in this bloody bone freezing God forsaken place . . . . He moaned again as I forced him back into an upright position back into his seat, but disturbing him in this manner meant having to physically touch various un-kept parts of him, his thick greasy black hair, clothes oosing with road grime. I heaved him upright and he slumped back into his position which sent a fresh wave of cheap lager up into my nostrils; he had been drinking steadily for a few hours which I could only presume was partly to amuse himself, partly to break up the monotony of the journey but mostly I decided, he was doing it just to scare me to death, whilst driving me to . . . . ? I really did not know; maybe to the end of my days; maybe to Lhasa; maybe to his Grandmas house; maybe to never never land;

who cares I thought to myself . . . . lets get out of here its bloody freezing . . . !

Finally after many kilometres the cheap low alcohol Asian lager must have frozen, distilled itself then doubled in volume as we doubled in altitude and at approximately 5600 meters his brain waved goodnight to the world and gracefully, irresponsibly . . . . collapsed at the wheel.

I reacted and grabbed the wheel, laughed out aloud to myself as a statement returned to my mind, to be careful what you wish for and yes I had no idea in my wildest imagination that I would be doing this. "Yes we know." I heard one of the more mischievous travel Gods answer, and I turned quickly to try to see him out of the corner of my mind, just to try to get a look at him, but he was too quick for me this time. When you are in a situation where you wished you were somewhere else, then normally this means you are having an adventure, this I reassured myself.

It was 2am I was driving a beat up old saloon car made up of various makes and models, the driver having passed out a while ago being too drunk to continue. I looked around at the interior, which was like that of a pimp daddy afro cosmic sixties flashback and was going to be my ride into oblivion I thought, why not lets go out in style, as we bounced over a road that I was sure was built as some sort of mechanical endurance test, rather than a convenient highway through Tibet . . . . ! Where the hell were we anyway? and still my altimeter kept climbing, 5000 meters and still bouncing, sliding, struggling to maintain momentum and traction climbing up through this winding dirt road. There were patches of sheet ice and holes in the road as though it had been blanket bombed. I struggled with the controls bouncing all over the place, the road was fighting me, wrenching the wheel from side to side whilst trying to avoid the really really bad bits, the deep ruts and holes with fear of getting stuck . . . . (again) many times we had lost the road or got into a patch of ice, mud or deep ruts and lost traction, whereby everyone had to stop, get out and push and pull the vehicle to get it free.

It had all started off quite normal I thought, as I started recalling the early hours of today, wow . . . . was it still today! had I been asleep and woke up in the same movie again? Well anyway it had all started out quite normal, apart from the guy who picked me up, who looked like some Tibetan Frank Zappa look-alike; I chuckled to myself recollecting that image. I tried to communicate to him as best I could because he seemed quite anxious at first bombarding me with a barrage of aggressive sounding questions, which all I could do in response was to smile and say "hey dude just take me as far as you can baby, be cool." Hoping he could read in between the lines somewhere, and bridge the language barrier, but eventually he relaxed and we settled down into the journey ahead together.

I tried to calculate in my mind roughly where we might be and when we would get to Markham but gave up trying to be so specific, lets just go with the flow we are going in the right direction.

We seemed to be driving for hours, and the road became very rough, whereby much of it was still being worked on and huge excavation was under way, cutting through the foreboding geology, therefore we were constantly in clouds of dust, very particular, very dry fine which easily found its way through any filtering system the car did not possess. It had a very particular smell as well, I can still remember it clearly after being with it for so many hours permeating through every hole and every pore, and have never come across it anywhere else before or since, layers of it rapidly built up inside my nostrils which became dry, sore, and my lungs ached for fresh air, every now and then I would heave and launch into sporadic fits of uncontrollable coughing. I think I sweated moon dust for the next few days.

After a few more hours we eventually arrived in a large town and came to a stop, Frank Zappa made an eating gesture. I get out and look around realizing this was not Markham that I was expecting. At this point I half expected to be sent off on the road again, or at any one of these places waiting for one of them to give me a sign that we have arrived, but there were no signs, no one said anything or even could do really and I was starting to really lose track of where we were and how far we had travelled. A few other cars pulled up behind ours and I got introduced to his colleagues, it looks like they all work together from noticing some sign writing on the cars all in Tibetan, they all seemed very close to each other, friendly, loyal and committed. I found it interesting to be in such alien surroundings and situations finding my instincts becoming sharper, looking for signs, looking for clues, pieces to the puzzle, looking for something to recognize, food, shelter, directions, friends or foe? Distant otherwise dormant compartments of our minds suddenly stimulated again, aware of being cushioned, comfortable, our instincts become lazy and off guard, cushioned with modern convieniences and only having to survive the native suburban hunter gatherers, snakes and ladders, maybe once in a while we get to reach the summit of metaphoric corporate mountains.

All eyes dance around the room, and I meet theirs one by one and smile waiting for someone to say something but no need, everyone was comfortable and more interested to be eating. One of them suddenly reaches into his bag and produces a plastic bag, and then with a heavy thud lands in the centre of the table. Hands grab at the contents of a chunk of what I presumed to be semi-cured or fossilised Yak meat wrapped around one of its major supporting bones. I was hungry, someone produced a knife and started slicing it up. I sunk my teeth into one that got passed my way; it had a musty, fatty taste that was, because of my hunger, almost but not quite enjoyable. I let my senses and imagination go over it thoroughly. I conjured up images of origin . . . big hairy Yak, removal, preparation and storage, the latter of which I did not want to think about for too long, but I think maybe it had been wrapped in an old pair of walking socks removed from the dead body of their last hitch hiker and then stored in the back of the pick up to bounce around and become naturally tenderized, then matured in the dusty heat of the midday Tibetan sun for numerous days or months. Yes I was sure of it.

All in all I felt very humble to be with them. I did not feel that sensation of being a foreigner that you often get sometimes, we were in a situation together and they wanted to help me out. Food arrived which consisted of a big pot of broth, which we scooped out and poured onto our bowl of noodles, this seemed to be the standard and cheapest way to eat in these parts. Together we noisily got stuck in, slurping and spitting out small pieces of bone on to the floor, belching afterwards and I smiled feeling very much at home. We finished and I tried to pay my share, but they would not let me humbling me even more. The compassion and friendliness continued through out the journey regularly offering me food and drink, with no sensation of pecking order or one better than the other feeling.

The road went on and on, many hours passed and I lost track of trying to calculate where, who, why and when just watching the crazy geology ahead unfold then flatten itself out under the wheels of this car. I started to notice Frank Zappa was looking agitated, shifting about in his seat, then looking at me. Maybe he was tired I thought, after all he had been driving a long while and who knows how much before I was picked up. Some time later after a long silence he pointed at the wheel, I reached over and tried to steady it thinking he wanted to look for something in the car, no he pointed to me and then the wheel again, "Ahhh . . . . you want me to drive?" Yes he was tired. We stopped and swapped places then I gently pulled away and he smiled, after some time he patted me and gave me the thumbs up obviously pleased with my driving and now felt he could relax whereby he closed his eyes and soon his mouth was catching flies. I thought it was again a good feeling of trust between two humans. It was also a strange feeling to be driving myself through China towards Tibet, that echo in my mind again telling me, "Yes I did not think I would be doing this today." With that thought I amused myself with the situation and took a mental photograph, one of many that comes flooding back as I write and recollect it all now still as rich and as vivid as if it was still happening, the memory of these moments and the power of our imagination is a beautiful thing and should be allowed full freedom with no limits. Turn off those TVs and chat shows there is much more going on outside without having to re invent any of it creating a brick prison for ourselves, broad casted, biased, media, propaganda, that we sit our children in front of God knows what is being broad casted deep into their sub consciousness . . . . ! Video games that teach to kill whilst smiling, suppressing the ability to communicate without pushing a button, conversation becomes boring too difficult, meal times that get forgotten until the next save point, families become individuals in their own alternative reality, lack of communication, lack of communion, we argue, we shout, we lose respect for each other, we have no class, no culture, no honour in the end, the chat shows, the dramas, the isms and schisms, designer label, better, bigger, more, must have better than you . . . . ! We seem to me to be a lost culture an empire that crushed, killed and raped to get what it wanted; exploiting other lands and homes creating slaves to feed our greed we have much to be ashamed about, much to be proud about, too much to do. Simple people, uneducated, savages, the ones on the streets with no clothes on their back they were the ones that gave me what they had, for no other reason but to help as one human to another human does it take so much suffering to become humble I wonder?

I felt humble, I felt ashamed at times, I thought about it all to much, and here I was taking my turn to drive my cargo of strange encounters. I watched as the day slowly became into night, relentlessly meandering the switch backs and pot holes, the road kept going on into the night, with absolutely no idea where I am. Were we still in China? We have been driving for so long maybe 9 hours now, and still no sign of this place Markam, it looked so close on my map, just the next town north of Dequin, if we really had not reached Markam then this is going to be one hell of a long road.

More hours passed driving as much as possible only stopping at a few places very briefly. We arrived in another large town and we drove around as though they were looking for something; I tried to ask what was happening and Frank just motioned to be calm. I got the impression something important was going on, maybe something to do with their business? Or maybe they forgot where they lived . . . ! I was getting very frustrated that I could not communicate anything at all and my brain was fading fast along with the night, the distance and this bloody long, dusty road was really tiring. I later realized in retrospect that one of these places must have been Markham but at the time I was so tired and disorientated it could have been on the moon for all I knew and certainly would have accounted for all the dust and bloody huge distance . . . . yes that was it, we had driven to the moon, I was sure of it; this was a secret Tibetan space station, somewhere, somehow we had managed to get lost and drove up a very large mountain pass to appear on the dark side of the moon, yeah . . . . this was not Tibetan any more this was lunar, that is why I could not understand anyone because they were all speaking some strange lunar language, and maybe their beer had special bubbles in it to account for the thin atmosphere . . . . yeah, yeah . . . . OK it was late and my mind was a little disorientated and various parts of it were offering alternative realities. I indulged them.

The endurance continued with what seemed like endless dusty roads, a roller coaster ride regularly reaching 4000 meters and then twisting down again. I cannot see anything, it is completely black outside and I am hunched forward as far as I can with the steering wheel in my chest trying to get a bit closer to the screen, gripping on for dear life, trying desperately to gain some visual advantage, having to squint through the wind shield that is thick with a sludge of yellowy brown lunar anthracite, candle like headlamps pathetically try to light the road ahead. My temples had been gradually thumping for the last hour or two, so I was relieved when we came to a stop outside what looked like a roadside café or moon base I had no interest to eat with what felt like a supernova like migraine coming on. I just wanted to lie down for a while and close my eyes, give my mind a rest, but there were too many questions flying around in there now that had developed into an unhealthy rhythm of repetitive potential madness, somewhere a hideous song was being thrashed out deep inside my temporal lobe, and although I desperately tried I could not see what was powering it, where the switch was to turn it off or even as a last resort, a gun to blow my brains out . . . . dam this headache, the long day, the distance and high altitude was starting to get to me and I felt all the colour fading out of me. I felt completely cold, drained and translucent white I felt that I was becoming invisible, fading into oblivion.

The time was now 10.30pm we had been driving for 11 hours. How far had we come? Were we in Tibet yet? Where were all the check points? it seemed as though we had been bouncing down a dirt track for thousands of kilometres and certainly my head felt that way. I motioned to Frank that I was feeling very tired and need to rest, he points to one of the other cars and shows me that I can move the seat and lay back. I surrendered myself to the seat and slumped into it like a corpse until the engine started up and we were off again. My head spun and stomach wrenched with the motion, so I tried to imagine that I just got upgraded to business class, whereby I could relax and put my feet up, maybe watch a movie, take a glass of wine and look at the cute air hostess . . . . forgetting myself and my manners; I abruptly bought myself out of delirium for a moment so that I could introduce myself to the driver, who was a young looking Tibetan guy, who was already a few inches too close, grinning from ear to ear peering at me with saucer like eyes, and looking very very very pleased with himself, no . . . . no, not pleased, just . . . . pissed . . . . WWW shit Nooooooo!!! . . . . Ptshhhhhhh . . . . he opened up another bottle of Dali beer and threw the empty in the rear with the rest of them! and then bombarded me with broken dialect of basically telling me what my name was about thirty seven times only pausing in between so that he could break out into a few minutes of 'lunar laughter' like any lunar-tic would whilst dribbling and nervously messing with every control in the car he could find and whilst all this was going on he still somehow managed to drive without looking at the road, mind you not that it made much difference because you could not see out of the windscreen anyway, and even if you could the candles in the headlamps needed replacing.

Ptshhhhhhhh . . . . went another bottle which waved goodbye to the passing full one as it passed go without collecting 200, by the time he got to the third one, his mood had become really excitable; he was singing at the top of his voice, bouncing up and down in his seat like some twisted Muppet creation, a jack in the box that could not make his mind up, whilst fumbling with a DVD player that was now playing some sort of Tibetan soft porn, Mr. pimp daddy we got it going on tonight with a one way ticket to disaster. He pointed at the wheel, "Oh oh" I thought, looks like I got to drive again. I was not really feeling up to it at all but with the condition he was in I thought I would feel a bit safer and that it would also give my mind something to focus on and maybe forget for a moment that it's actually trying to escape out of my skull!

We swapped places and I paddle the gear lever around like a big pudding spoon trying to find a usable gear; 1st . . . . wow, that was a lucky guess, but trying to work this with an accelerator pedal that was somehow set to either flat out or off; I consequently wheel spun out of there and started climbing up into the icy heavens. Many more hours passed by of these bloody long, dusty, icy, dirt roads. Mr. Lunar-tic is completely in his own world now still singing track number 2 whilst we have moved on to track 9. The situation had rapidly developed into what was the worst scenario possible for a headache; of which I felt was soon about to develop into an inner lobe super nova. I did not know how much longer my mind would be able to support any more trauma and I was sure it would soon collapse in on itself forming a dark pool of throbbing turbulence; and would have laughed a little more at the extremity of it all, if it did not hurt so much.

I looked around at the interior of the car; it was pimped up like a full on gangster Tibetan rap fanny magnet full with, fur, dangling things, plastic bags of clothes, biscuits, crisps. The DVD player was blasting out some sort of Asian, acid hip hop rap, psychedelic porn, thrash metal. I think this guy actually lived in here, it was like your first room that you rented as a student, but by now I was getting bored about it all, or traumatized more like it, my mind was about to form a new solar system after first collapsing . . . . Please when will this road end? When will it stop? Where is my bed? Will I ever sleep again?

I had to stop several times as more bottles of Dali beer were exchanged with some of the other drivers, then several more times after that for them to empty themselves of it all . . . . weak beer, yes but once inside an Asian metabolism the transformation is rapid, unpredictable and very scary . . . . I think the biology of their genetics somehow alchemically turns it into a hallucinogenic class A, triple distilled lager, brain, giggling, dribbling, substance capable of transforming the ugliest girl into the most beautiful porn star ever imagined, the finale is a total blissed out experience whereby they keep telling you how much they love you until they throw up and pass out . . . . !

One of them did pass out, but luckily did not throw up. At some God forsaken high altitude we had to stop again, more pissing, then tried to set off again but the car ahead just stayed, we waited a while there until someone eventually got out to see what was wrong; the problem was with the driver, he was asleep, simply passed out, the weak alcohol mixed with high altitude and the even more sensitive Asian genetics had finally got the better of him, one down three to go!!! His friends proceeded to remove him into the passenger seat and signalled me to drive, well OK at least I might get some peace. I get into the aforementioned car and I push his head away from the gear lever where it had slumped. I tried to select and engage a gear frantically stirring the gear lever around in ever increasing larger circles until finally . . . . clunk . . . . I found one. I gently pressed the accelerator but the motor screamed, until the valves were bouncing and then let the clutch out and wheel spun off into the freezing night once more. It felt like my mind was in some sort of constant loop accompanied by a constant thump from my inside temples; like a Viking battle ship that was inside my head boom boom boom boom . . . . 'ramming speed' . . . . there seemed to be no way out of it, like the record was stuck until we would finally run out of able drivers . . . . !

I checked the altimeter, it registered 4700m and still this road to hell was climbing, my head was spinning, the veins inside my temples were pounding with each Viking battle drum beat within them, still climbing, bouncing, sliding, wheel spinning. We were now at 5000 meters it was about 2.00am and inside the car had become noticeably arctic; the heater was useless and was just blowing freezing air around but nothing else . . . . hell had frozen over in here. I could see patches of sheet ice outside all over the road glinting in the dim headlamps beneath a clear sky, which I could now just see a few bright stars far away in deep freezing space, here I did not feel so far away from.

Lunar-tic No. 2 is still out cold so at least I had some sort of peace. I gazed through the windscreen trying to keep up and follow the dim tail lights ahead, but the conditions were getting worse, the deep ruts in the ice were becoming harder and harder to avoid. Then I feel the car suddenly drop through the ice and I instinctively give it some more gas to keep the momentum up, wheels lost traction and spin out of control, the car is thumping, crashing up and down in and out of deep ruts, engine is screaming trying to make it through. I feel and hear the engine bashing against the bulkhead, and imagine that there must be just one good engine mounting bracket left and the rest must be either missing or detached. I feel we are in some sort of off road endurance challenge. My eyes desperately want to close, someone is stabbing my temples with a dagger, altitude, throbbing, nausea . . . . I wanted to vomit and felt darkness closing in, beads of pre-vomit cold sweat forming on my forehead. I lose concentration and in that instance I suddenly see the tail lights on top of me; I brake hard so as to not hit the back of him and I slide into a deep rut, shit . . . . this time I am stuck. I try desperately backwards, then forwards slowly sinking lower and lower until I accept I cannot get out. I reluctantly get out, as I open the door a blast of Himalayan air took my breath away, it must be well below—20 at least. We push and shove and swear and curse this thing out of there, leaving me rasping for breath in this thin atmosphere and a sickening pressure pounding inside my head. I get back inside the car hoping this would be the last time, but it was to be a regular routine from now on, the road was well above 5000 meters and became impossible not to get stuck in which several times we had to do the same routine. The cars had been taking such a hammering I could not imagine why anyone would want to come this way. I was thinking something bad was sure to happen and this is just totally crazy, its just a matter of time luck was overdue thinking: 1) Either we get stuck here and freeze to death 2) Enough parts are going to finally fall off these cars until they all destroy themselves and we all freeze to death 3) We all fall asleep and drive over the side of a mountain to our doom . . . .

Number three decided to happen first . . . . I watched in disbelief as the tail lights in front start to make some strange manoeuvres, first slowing up as though to stop, then speeding up again, veering to one side then the other, suddenly speeding off again and I am thinking he is just messing me around or what! Then suddenly takes a kamikaze dive to the left, keeps going left . . . . I cant believe it . . . . the car goes over the side, in slow motion at first, then as gravity took over the red tail lights that I was transfixed upon, suddenly just dropped out of sight, shit . . . . is there a big drop? I don't know it just goes over and disappears. I dread to think, my mind freezes.

My heart was suddenly trying to leave my rib cage, shock then terrible realization that something really bad must have happened. I felt a surge of adrenalin and then a chemical rush, my eyes became open wide like saucers and gazed into the void trying to see if there were any signs of life. I get out, it's bloody freezing outside I shiver and my teeth start to chatter uncontrollably. I walk towards a black precipice, my legs are like jelly and stumble over rock and ice to see over the side. I expected to see a black void and was sure there would be no sign of the car, but as I gingerly peered over the side, incredibly, I see the tail lights about 50 meters below, and the car teetering at an acute angle with its front embedded into a large rock which luckily had broke its fairground final destination ride to . . . . is there a God?

If he had gone over anywhere else along this way it would have been sure death, but just here was a rocky ledge below the road, a very lucky escape. Maybe these Buddhists were right in some of their thinking, and it was not their time to go this time!

The driver was fine, although a little shaken up afterwards by the slap he got from his colleague, whose car it belonged to! who was now frantically waving his arms around and obviously saying how the bloody hell are we going to get my van out of here?

So . . . . 5400 meters up well below—20, silly O clock in the bloody freezing Tibetan morning . . . . I was thinking, phone the AA, phone a friend, phone God . . . . I don't care any more I want my bed, where is that? Shit my head is pounding again, this is just unbelievable torture. I need to descend, I need to sleep, I need to get warm.

One thing about Asians once they get an idea into their head you cannot budge them, and believe me they were determined to somehow get this van back on the road, rebuilt, re-sprayed and driving again. I did not even consider it; after giving it a quick look over I quickly realised there is no way, no way definitely . . . . its fucked. Leave it.

There was no way I thought that anyone would even try to attempt it, how were you going to try to drive it back up to the road 50 meters up? I was in no condition to even try to think about, the thought of it send new waves of pain surging through small reserves of well being, all I could do was to observe, I would try to help in anyway I could and was hoping that if I went to sleep it would help them a great deal. Maybe one of them was some sort of Buddhist enlightened being capable of lifting impossible things just with his mind.

What seemed like hours passed of head scratching, moving rocks, kicking things to no avail and unfortunately no feats of spiritual phenomena occurred. Finally just as everything had nearly gone numb, and I mean literally everything! A decision seemed to have been reached and some sort of action was taking place. No! . . . . I watched in disbelief as they continued to move stone and debate between themselves, until I gathered what they were trying to do. It seemed that they were trying to clear a way to make a sort of slip road up to the road above, out came shovels and a pick, these people were unbelievably motivated . . . my mind just somersaulted in disbelief. I helped the best I could as there was nothing else left for me to do except freeze, so I started to lift rocks, to clear the way but after walking and lifting for just a few seconds I was so out of breath, having to stop rasping at the icy air reminding myself that yes of course we were very high, my temples pounded again as I waited to re gain breath, when is this night going to end?

Maybe two hours passed, we finished the slip way and it actually started to look like it could work, we had made a clear run to a flat area below from where the car was stuck, then it was just a steep run up to the road above, that I was not sure a 4by4 would handle let alone a front wheel drive van! We all gathered around the front of the van to try to push it away, and a big cheer let out as we released the car from its rocky grip, re assembled behind it and then pushed in unison with the poor engine that was screaming its pistons off, as it then tried to go up the slip way we had cleared, but no way, even for these motivated, spiritually assured Asians they had to finally lose face and give up, but I was really impressed by their determination and to be honest it nearly bloody well worked . . . . !

Lunar-tic No.3 got a final slap and so with one vehicle down, two drivers down, with two more left to go, we were running out of drivers and vehicles and they way the remaining vehicles had been abused trying to get us over this mountain pass, I don't think these last two were too far off from their final destination.

I returned back to the saloon hybrid that I was driving but noticed it sitting a bit low at the front end, and then realised . . . shit its got a flat . . . my mood that had just been elevated at the thought of driving out of here suddenly committed suicide and leapt over the crevasse into the void leaving an empty shell—20 desolate feeling in my mind, all that was left was the sensation of a jack hammer that was now trying to break through my skull . . . .

Putain du merd . . . . encore du merd . . . . and other French obscenities, I cannot believe this endless night. My mind still suicidal but now committed to despair for the rest of its mortal existence, until calmly it just accepted defeat and its fate never to be at peace or at rest again. I began to enjoy a moment of total despair which gave the authority for denial to rule and in that moment of blankness, it was peaceful, until a few synapses fired up from within a small infrequently used compartment of my mind, where logic was once created; I recognized its voice from when I used to take notice of it, when I used to make plans, when I used to think . . . . it said . . ."you know what you got to do so just get on with it, stop feeling sorry for yourself . . . you are having an adventure." Great advice, perfect, thank you . . . . I threw the master switch back to off again. Replaced the out of order sign and wrote another beware of the yeti do not enter.

I helped to change the wheel, and lift the body up because there was no where in the mud to put a jack, even if they had one! but thank God they did have a spare wheel. Pessimistically I went through a list one by one of a hundred things that I expected to happen next, but the wheel nuts did come undone, did not snap in the freezing conditions, the spare was inflated and was the correct size, no one else passed out, we did not get attacked by rabid snow leopards or suffer multiple frost bite whereby certain sensitive areas would need amputation.

We were actually about to set off again driving out of here, aaahhh what a shame I was just starting to get comfortable and familiar with all this suffering, the path to enlightenment as they say . . . . oh well all good things have to come to an end, lets go . . . . I excitedly ram it into first and floor this tin, Tibetan Ragga muffin out of there.

Finally we are in convoy again and moving, hammering these vehicles over this ridiculous terrain I was a little relieved not to be able to see how high we were or the inevitable precipice that must be waiting for one of us to make another mistake, but also kind of curious to have been denied a clear view and to see our surroundings which I imagined must be pretty spectacular, instead it had felt like I had been playing a video game for the past 24 hours starring at a monitor and thrashing the steering wheel from side to side.

We started to descend and after some time I started to feel the pressure release its vice like grip on my temples, the nausea in the pit of my stomach dissipated and left with a sensation of blankness, numb, my mind had flat lined and now all systems had been shut down then re started in safe mode, leaving me with a less than basic ability to function, my hands turned the wheel according to some other automated response, my mind and body feels separate to one another and I sit and stare into the darkness from within my own shell as the barrage of motion and turbulence continue. Suddenly I am seeing things, red lights in front, lots of them. I brake and slide and come out of my driving trance to see many tail lights of cars, trucks and a coach, not moving, queuing up at now maybe 4.30 am, what now? It looked like we could be entering civilization and I see a few trees, telegraph poles, fences, maybe it was a check post? shit I had forgot all about that whilst my mind was preoccupied with surviving, a backlog of reality suddenly caught up and smacked me in the back of my head . . . . Baaam, reality check post. I was driving as an illegal alien with an unconscious passenger of unknown criminal record, stinking of alcohol and all of us covered in dust, mud and snot . . . . well at least I looked like and could be passed as a Tibetan now, but it would still be pretty hard to explain all this in this strange hour to unforgiving Chinese police. The best I hoped for now was a nice cold prison cell for a few hours, morning or whatever time it should not have been. I relished the thought of a prison cell, a hard cold bed to lie down on, no more driving. Aaaaah bliss.

We stopped and waited but nothing moved maybe twenty minutes, everyone completely spent now hoping that something would just happen and start moving again so as not to have to get out into the cold again. I had no warm blood left in me at all and nothing inside me to heat any of it up again. I really did not want to move. I see a truck start to manoeuvre, it reverses but I cant quite see what the trouble is, then it bounces like crazy and slides to one side so presume it must be ice and mud, it tries a run up this time but again a big cloud of diesel bellows out as it powers through, bounces like crazy again and starts to slide, keeps sliding, nearly sideways and then grinds to a halt, shit . . . . if this huge thing got stuck I cant see us having a chance. It makes a second attempt, takes a slightly different route, bounces like crazy again, almost stops then somehow finds grip and makes it through. We get out to see the road, yes its really bad, a huge sheet of ice completely over the road with deep mud underneath, deep ruts where wheels had broken through creating big holes where they had ground to a halt.

We wait and wait and finally one by one as they find better ground they all make it through, but we are all drained now completely non functional, cold, tired and defeated with no energy and cannot face having to push and pull vehicles if they get stuck in the ice, we decided to rest a while and try to sleep a little until the daylight breaks through in a few hours.

I find as many things as I can to cover myself with from within the car to try to get warm, paper, boxes, hat, gloves and try to sleep; it is still bloody freezing and soon my unconscious friend is making deep unpleasant noises from the back of his throat like someone had slit it. I started to laugh a little then guilt came over me and I started to feel a bit concerned; maybe he could actually be dying? With the alcohol and freezing conditions, his body temperature could drop down too low, maybe his throat was collapsing! it certainly sounded like it! I kicked him, very compassionately of course, and he responded very well . . . . silence. With that diagnosis and my own karma restored I relaxed and tried to sleep A blurry sensation of time passed, maybe two hours in and out of consciousness getting more and more cold, trying to wrap myself up with two inches of cloth that I am clutching on to. Finally, too cold and frustrated that sleep had been and gone; I decided to get up, very soon everyone else started stirring, moaning, groaning, farting. Outside the first signs of light were just starting to show, a new day that gave rise to more options and a huge relief to see that this endless night was coming to an end, finally . . . . but to where . . . ?

I get out of the car to stretch stiff and aching body parts and went over to look at the road with the others, it looked even worse in the light, deep mud underneath an insubstantial layer of ice, also the whole road was on a slight angle so if you started to slide you would end up in a huge ditch at the side of the road. I stay and watch as the first car tries an attempt at it. A cloud of smoke bellows out of its exhaust and lurches forward; it looks like they decided the best tactics is to get a good run up and hit it as fast as you can, so this next guy, he nails it to the floor and hits the ice just as he manages to engage second gear, the engine screaming, pistons slapping and tappets tapping. I laugh as it hits the ice and pathetically takes a nose dive through the surface, steam rising up from the bonnet like huge storm clouds, the front of the car buries its nose down deep into the mud. I expected to see it come to an abrupt stop there and then, but somehow it managed to keep up its momentum, whilst its front springs were fully compacted, or probably both now protruding through the wheel arches into the engine bay somewhere, then suddenly released its tension and the front end sprang skywards like a pimped up air suspension; it screamed slid, spat, swore, coughed and then kicked up a big lump of road behind it; then in true Tibetian style, shook itself off and casually emerged out the other side singing: "Naaaa nothing to it, easy peasy" It rasped, there was a brief silence then everyone cheered and ran up to the driver like he had just won the Paris Dakar rally. With this technique approved, the rest of the cars followed suit and all made it through, it was like the final challenge we had broken through into the new frontier, the new world, the forbidden land, we were inside Tibet. Bloody hell . . . !

Now I sit caked in dust, mud and snot, still trying to recover some body heat and recollect the events over the last 24 hours. How? what? why? when? I was on a bus and actually on my way to Lhasa. It was incredible after the ordeal of the mountain death pass drive to oblivion, these guys dropped me off in some strange town, found a bus station for me and after speaking with the bus driver I was allowed on and paid 2500 Yuan, I still couldn't believe it. I wondered how far away I was and tried to calculate how long we had been driving, thinking maybe we covered 350 km, so maybe another good day on this bus and we will be there. Hmmmmmm a wave of doubt swept over me, after everything that had just happened suddenly it all felt too easy, maybe its a trap? Do they really know where I want to go? Maybe its going back to China? I catch the attention of some children playing close by and ask them: "gong gong chee cher, chee Lhasa" Which is what my Chinese dictionary had suggested, hoping they understood me "bus go Lhasa?" They nod so I tried to relax. I look around at my surroundings again to confirm with my mind, yes this does look like a bus and it is confirmed by a small boy that does not understand me that it is actually going to Lhasa, what can go wrong? maybe there will be check points here; my mind would not relax it was preparing itself for the next set back, but I reassure it and for now lets just enjoy the ride and see where we get to next!

Tuesday...
New Years Eve,
A Police Station,
Somewhere In Tibet

Please Divide By Zero

Chapter 9

"No I don't know how I got here or which road I took, you probably wouldn't believe me even if I did know" I desperately tried to explain to my captor whilst his Cold eyes scanned me up and down like a bar code and then peered deep into my deceitful western soul.

He was a big man, proudly uniformed and addressed me sternly with a cold official approach. I tried not to be intimidated, tried to look relaxed and lighten the mood a little by saying: "So am I in trouble then?" No emotion at all just a stark reply: "You will be fined."

He sounded more like a Cyborg from Dr Who.

"You will be assimilated, you will comply."

I had my travelling money but I did not budget for any hefty fines, or any fines at all for that matter so already in my mind I denied all charges and was prepared to tell them I had no way of paying, that I was just hitch hiking and got a little lost on my way to Nepal, which was basically all true.

So there I was sat in the police headquarters of the alien processing department waiting for my passport to be returned so that I could go to the bank and change a little currency for my release. The officer in charge of this department was immersed in some important work and I could not seem to get his attention; he was in another dimension deep within his computer screen; I could hear the clunk click, lock and load, then followed a barrage of heavy gauge artillery fire, arms, legs, heads, blood and guts spilling all over the monitor, he was loving it, ripping it up, eyes fixed, fully dilated and beads of high body count sweat started forming on his brow. I cleared my throat and try to gain his attention again, several times in fact, until finally I managed to interrupt his lunch time genocide just long enough to ask if I could have my passport back. He stared at me for a nano second, which was long enough for him to instinctively assess and target all my available fatal hit zones. I sensed an intrusion of my more venerable parts and tactically slid sideways towards a sturdy looking roof pillar, from which I peered my head around to ask again, "Err . . . . please sir . . . . err, you think I could have my passport back pleeeeeeeeease?"

Maybe he was a little disappointed that I had interrupted him during a particularly high body count and abruptly pointed towards the door that was marked in big, red, stern looking Chinese characters, hmmmmmmmm I take that as a no then? Baaam . . . . both barrels exploded and the massacre continued without my passport!

To rewind a little; a few hours prior to these events I was comfortably uncomfortable on a bus, and after passing three or four checkpoints, my paranoia of being an illegal alien was starting to subside. I started to accept that the worst was over and I was going to make it to Lhasa after all. I beamed from ear to ear as I recollected in disbelief the events leading up to the present moment. Flashbacks of crazy images kaleidoscoped through my mind, of cars, ice, mud, grinning toothless crazy drunk Tibetans, tail lights in the night and high mountain passes. I felt rich inside and humble to be here, maybe various Gods were smiling upon me after their intervention and pleased that they had got me here, in their own way, maybe to amuse themselves and or maybe to teach me something. I am not sure, except I felt good, here amongst all these local Tibetans all on their way to pay homage to their faith, to be in the belly button of the world, Lhasa. Many of them looked like they were wrapped in rags and clutching bundles of food for the road, maybe this was a once in a lifetime journey for some of them, and here I was just doing it for my own amusement or stupidity? It was more than that for me though, I respected these people and their faith, their courage, they were also on a journey with different challenges, but for me it was the journey not the destination, the highs and lows that was my pilgrimage, the effort and the reward, the lessons it will teach me, maybe that was my faith. I was on my own spiritual journey but I had no way of giving it form or a name, it was more important for it to remain anonymous as I felt it needed to be. Infinite and therefore formless. I had my own faith that things would turn out fine as long as I did my part of the deal, try to keep some sort of karma intact.

Hours passed; I relaxed and started to feel a familiar warm, wrapped up in cotton wool feeling. A blanket of fatigue wrapped its huge arms around me and saturated my being. I had no reason to fight it this time and I let myself slip into its coma like canopy. Dreamily I dozed. In and out of consciousness I daydreamed and sporadically glimpsed the darkness of the night blur past the window of the bus. Abstract images of hard, frozen shapes and rocky skyscrapers blurred past in a hypnotic dance of reality and memory, past, present and future all blurred into one video, streaming past my vision. Finally one by one various senses faded and switched off, lights, camera, action, Ptzzzzzzzzz, nothing, peace, oblivion . . . .

I wake suddenly after what felt like seconds later with a woman prodding me, my mind is still far, far away and it does not want to come back, refusing to acknowledge any engaging situation.

"Bleeeeh? What's happening?" I think to myself.

I look around and everyone else is settled and comfortable, so why am I being prodded? Leave me alone! She insists with me. I cannot understand anything, arrrrrgh I did not want to wake up like this, slowly bits of information and reality creep in and my logic compartment starts to process the bits of the puzzle . . . . its still night time, no one else is moving, the woman wants me to get up. She points to my bag and to outside.

"Are we here?" I ask. "Lhasa?" It looks just like any old town. I check the time, its 1.00 am, no its too early there should be at least another days ride yet, shit what's happening? someone speaks; "Lhasa tomorrow, you sleep hotel now, go Lhasa tomorrow." Confused but with no other choice I have to comply, they obviously know what I need to do, and two others now are also getting off, so at least I am not being singled out. I was starting to worry that they had got nervous and decided to eject me somewhere. I sort of learn from the other couple in broken English that we have to stay here for the night at a hotel, then tomorrow take another bus to Lhasa. I did not understand where the bus was going now or where and how we go tomorrow? My mind and soul still felt battered and bruised so I found it all too hard to think about, so I didn't and just dreamily followed and walked into the lobby of a nearby hotel; slightly disappointed at being disturbed from a very deep, much needed sleep and now having a mountain of unanswered questions building up again, that no one was going to be able to answer, well only time will tell.

I could feel a restless night coming on, with too many questions flying around inside my mind, someone said they would ring me in the morning but could not explain why, or what would happen.

Finally I pushed the questions to one side and managed to sleep a little but I wake up early, before my alarm went off, after having a stressful night wrestling with bed sheets and feeling strangely too comfortable, all this time I had been camping or staying in the cheapest rooms I could find; I sort of got used to those conditions and now this way over budget room with working TV, a heater, glazed windows, a whole panel of buttons that I amused myself with for a few minutes by switching everything on, sheets that smelled and looked clean, and silence, was almost deafening, suffocating, the comfort actually made me uncomfortable.

I moodily kicked the sheets off on to the floor and with eyes half open, shuffled to the bathroom to freshen up. The shower felt good though and one luxury I would always wish to have; I forgot how long it had been, whilst travelling through China it had been too cold to even dare expose any part of my body, so I did not bother too much with hygiene. The brown stream of mud and filth verified this and history washed itself down the plug hole.

At 8.00am the phone rang and someone tried to tell me what was happening, but it was all in Chinese, but eventually I hear something recognizable; "Lhasa, you go now" With that I thank them and hurry down to the lobby. I check out and wait to see if anything else happens, but no, nothing, and I was starting to get nervous again. No one else comes down, no one seems to know where I am to go or even what I am doing here . . . . looks like its going to be another interesting day!

I was expecting the couple from the night before to come down and maybe we all travel together. I try to ask at the desk but they seem sure I was to go outside, therefore confused I walk outside and see that there is a bus station right next to the hotel, "aha." I think to myself, the missing piece to the puzzle, a little disappointed though as I presumed the ticket I paid for was actually going to get me to Lhasa.

My mind scrambled about a bit looking inside myself for other missing pieces of information, and turned them around, swapped them about a bit, tried to hammer the corners in place that I was sure should fit, but I was just eluding myself. Eventually I could only form one other alternative, maybe a bus was going to arrive here to pick up people from the hotel and continue, or the more obvious, but the one which I really did not want to believe; was that this was the end of the ride and I had to get another ticket from here.

I stood around for a while waiting for another alternative to manifest itself, my mind was on strike and protesting about the conditions it had to work under, so I could not come up with anything better.

I entered the bus station and tried to ignore all the faces that immediately turned and were now starring at me as though I had got a big sign on my head. I tried to imagine I was just an ordinary Tibetan on my way to Lhasa and tried to blend in, well my clothes were the same colour as theirs but I still stood out like a sore thumb. Gingerly I went up to the ticket counter and asked:

"Could I have a ticket pleeeeeeeeesa to La . . . ."

"no!"

She cut me off in mid sentence. I could see it in her eyes as she recoiled and ran away to the opposite side of her office trying to pretend what I asked for did not happen, several times I tried and I waited, waved money around and tried to buy a ticket, no one would acknowledge me. In a slightly confused state I walked away. I was stranded in a bus station. I looked around trying to catch the attention of anyone, but they all seem aware of exactly what is going on yet no one wants to intervene; eventually a young guy gestures me to wait. I use a little sign language with him and try to get him to buy a ticket for me, but he seems to be saying and pointing to the ticket office that . . . .

"They phone police" . . . .

"what! . . . . OK that's it, I am out of here."

I will hitch hike. I suddenly decided; just as I was about to leg it out of there, he tells me to wait and pulls out a mobile phone and he makes a call, gestures me to wait. I am nervous and I toy with the idea of just legging it now and walking, my instincts say go but something tells me I can trust this guy.

Ten minutes later I see a policeman walk in, shit I don't believe it I think he has turned me in. I get ready to leg it before I am noticed, but he takes my arm and tells me: "it ok, he my friend." Eh! He comes up and suddenly I see they know each other, they greet, then my friend turns to the ticket office and gives them the bird, Wow, cool! I have the law on my side then, my mood picks itself up off the floor and I shake his hand "shi shi" Thank you, but the officer does not smile, just asks for my papers. I see the expression of his friend now also looking a little confused. He takes my passport and examines it, then with no words he just points to the door and I have to follow, but I already know the inevitable, never trust a cop . . . . !

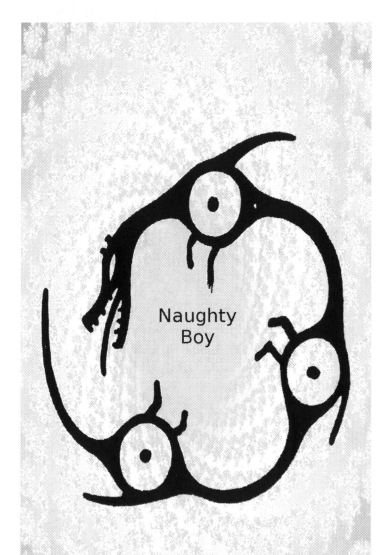

Chapter 10

The first hour inside the alien's entry and exit department of the police station was spent going over precise locations of where I had been since arriving in Tibet. I couldn't help noticing the sign on the wall where it said EXIT . . . .

. . . . Yes Please!

They asked me again and again how I got here and where I had travelled from. OK I thought to myself best just keep it sketchy as possible. I explained that I had been travelling from Thailand, Laos then into China, hitch hiking and hoping to get to Nepal, which was all true.

An official and stern voice replied: "Do you know your visa is out of date by 1 day, and that you have travelled through 5 restricted areas closed to foreigners."

"Whoops, really." I said, but inside I was kind of impressed, proud even, what a great achievement.

I was genuinely surprised though that my Chinese visa was out of date, as I specifically remember asking for a longer one when I applied for it in Thailand, but made the mistake of not checking it when I received it. I looked at it again in disbelief and it was indeed out of date. I had made a mistake and told him I would have applied for an extension if I had realized. I tried to look humble and hoped this appealed to his compassionate Buddhist nature; realizing my fate though was in their hands I therefore apologized and asked what could be done; "Could I apply for an extension and get a travel permit so that I could continue on to Nepal?" He did not answer but then began to sort of dictate to me as though he was reading from a list of crimes about to condemn my soul to eternal suffering: He started to list a break down of all the rules and regulations that I had broken and then repeated I had travelled through 5 restricted areas, he then went on to say that I was to write down on a piece of paper exactly what he had just told me then to say in my own words that I recognized these terrible crimes, that I was very, very, very sorry, was not allowed to apply for an extension, that I was to be grateful to all the officers present for their leniency towards me; because they had just decided and were willing to offer me a 7 day travel permit so that I could continue to Nepal, only upon after paying a 50 Euro fine; providing I did not stop; do not pass go and go directly to Nepal. Whatever humble pie game this was being played did not matter; this was a pretty good deal in the end.

I wrote in my humblest of handwriting everything they wished to hear; maybe he wanted to frame it and keep it as some sort of trophy. I felt it was some sort of test, like a show of face. I had to lose face there was no doubt about that, so with my defeat and my signed confession the mood seemed to be lightened; obviously pleased with this victory , his trophy, and he even seemed cheerful now.

With that over with I was sure I would be on my way again, now that I was armed with all the relevant paper work and could officially buy bus tickets, travel legally and relax a little, but a mountain of paper work followed, 12 documents, statements, detailed descriptions, of where, when, why, who, signed, triplicates, thumb printed, photographed it went on for so long that we had to break for lunch and was led to the police canteen for a short interlude. I had not eaten properly for a few days and so this part of the ordeal was very much welcomed. I walked into a canteen room and all eyes were upon me from the other officers but they were cool and just curious. I waved at them all, joked a little and they smiled.

The Chinese and Tibetans have incredibly noisy eating habits, and they don't seem to talk much when food is around and just get on with devouring bowls full of mostly, unrecognisable lumps of things that the noodles were trying to do their best to swim away from, making the chop stick chase even more of a challenge; I was stabbing at them for a while which I was quite happy to do because I wanted to help the noodles out a bit as they looked a bit stressed out and out-numbered, until someone came and offered me a spoon. I joined in with the orchestra of slurping and spitting out bones on to the floor or passing dogs or small children and found it comfortable in the end not to be so self conscious, it was good to slurp and chew and spit out anything you did not want on to the floor or anywhere else you felt inspired to spit at, it was normal here, it made me think what is normal anyway?

We finished our food but as I was still not a free man yet officially, my Tibetan captor asked me if I wanted to come with him on his duty whilst they continued to process the ridiculous amount of paper work; to extend my visa and grant me a travel permit. He was definitely more chilled out now, and seemed more human now that all the formalities were over with. He asked me if I was a Christian, which was a common question that I am asked by various people and nationalities, they don't know what we believe in or find it strange how many of us in the west do not have any faith, or grow rice, or have seven wives and fifty children . . . ! For them this is very strange, everyone believes in something don't they? Well I explained that many people where I came from do not believe in anything but for me I like look at it all with interest and an open mind. The conversation then turned towards Buddhism, as he was a devout follower and something which I find very peaceful and contains many truthful observations of nature and the nature of our minds, balance and harmony, through meditation and understanding which ultimately leads to enlightenment, peace and release from human suffering, the weaknesses we have to fight, desire, greed and complicated lifestyles being key elements that trap us and is the cause of much of our unhappiness. I couldn't agree more. Less is more for sure, travelling like this with just a bag, my tent and something to cook; I never really miss anything apart from family and friends in fact I feel I have more somehow there is an expansion of spirit and a heightened appreciation of simplicity.

Love, light and peace, yes we are all connected in some intricate web of cause and effect, so I shook hands with my capture and that was my Karma I suppose. I thought about all that and reflected upon it for a moment, everything happens for a reason. Well maybe I was lucky they caught me here and not much later at the border to Nepal? Maybe by then I would have been a week out of date with my visa and a much bigger trouble to follow and fine, yes count these days as lucky. I still get to see Lhasa without all the hassle of dodging uniforms and it had been an interesting encounter with the police here, they were OK in the end.

I have never been good with dealing with bits of paper, unless it meant drawing pictures on them, the ones with all these rules, regulations and demands. I have always hated those, not for want of being a rebel as I never mean anyone any harm, it's just something that I have always felt to the core of my soul is wrong, its gotten too complicated and stressful and I recoil away from it all in disgust, leaving me wanting to run away and hide. I don't know why it has never felt normal for me. In my world there are no rules there is no need for them, rules were only made because of other people who have darkness and fear in their hearts.

Meanwhile back at the station, it took 4 people all day to complete the paper work. I thought the French were bad for formalities but these guys seemed to have invented it. Finally I left at 6.00pm with my passport and just had to return the following morning for the travel permit to be issued. I booked into a room and tried to get my thoughts back on track again, but somehow I felt violated like the purity and the freedom of travel had been compromised from all this paperwork, pride, ego and bullshit, all this man power, paper work, expense, and waste of time for what? All I want to do is travel from here to there across this planet that should not really have to belong to anyone, why we have to be so possessive, greedy, and suspicious? there should be certain rights for people who are nomadic or wish to be nomadic, free to travel, to traverse this beautiful planet, that I am sure if God exists this would be in his original design too! Just greed and fear in the hearts of others and we have lost paradise, we fell from grace as they say.

Later on I was dropped off at a cheap hotel. Settled down inside my half way house and switched on the TV. I started to take notice of the news and quickly fell off my romantic travelling cloud, as I watched some program that was reviewing various problems from around the globe, graphically comparing each country side by side, so many problems, so much despair. I felt sad at the short sightedness and inevitability of it all, so much out of balance, so much wealth, so much power, so many resources, knowledge, materials, objects, and yet something like 800 million people still starving in the world, its madness. I talked with the officer today, there was a moment when he suddenly came over all solemn; something must have provoked, maybe my presence, a thought welled up inside him and he asked me what I thought about the state of the world, that there are so many problems did I think there would ever be a "One world." He said with much sincerity and sadness; I felt he hoped that I would tell him something positive from my part of the world, what he wanted to hear, hoped to hear. I replied as best I could: "I believe it is spiritually possible but politically impossible" For me I think there is too much greed and power in the world for spirituality to enter; we do not work as one yet still too many prejudices, too much manipulation and propaganda. We build our little empires, high fences and walls and shut the doors on those who fall. Keep everything to ourselves do not want to share, more of the more, bigger and better than you attitude.

"Mans happiness and gladness lies in his struggle and the most valuable kind is to struggle for his ideals"

I don't know who said this but it was a sticker that I noticed that was on the side of the kettle in the police station, it seemed to strike a chord and the kettle struggled to make a particularly great cup of tea that day.

The next morning was clear and cold as was every day. I could not believe my luck so far I had not seen a cloud in the sky for at least two months and I kind of got complacent about it expecting the same blue canopy overhead. It was such a beautifully crystal clear morning, even grey concrete seemed to have an elevated sense of clarity and definition, which reflected my mood as I walked into the police station.

I beamed and cheerfully waved at them all and beamed even more when my travel permit was handed to me. I promptly hurried out of there eager to be on my way to the nearest bus station.

This time I felt confident and walked smugly up to the counter, "tash dilek." . . . . Which I hoped this time translated to something like: "Greetings may all the Gods bless you with many children and grant you blessing from Buddha to end the eternal suffering of birth death and re birth so that you go directly to a higher level of existence, oh and by the way . . . . Chee chu Lhasa, gong gong chee cher Lhasa . . . . can I have a ticket to Lhasa . . . . Pleeeeeeeeeease!"

There was a long pause.

I let her do the usual blank look thing and waited to just before she was about to run away and hide in the corner, then smugly I produced my magic scroll with the sacred inscriptions; there were plenty of large red Chinese characters here to impress anyone. I waved it around a little and offered it up to the counter for her to examine, she gingerly took it from me and began to examine it suspiciously, then went off to converse with her colleagues, who looked at it under a better light, flicked through some pages of a book, returned to her ticket machine and looked around to see if anyone was watching her, and paused for too long, her hand was hovering over the issuing ticket button and stayed there for an uncomfortable amount of time until I could not take it anymore . . . .

"Arrrrrgh . . . . just press the bloody button will you"

I blurted out in my mind, but seeing that she had been conditioned and brainwashed from birth never to issue tickets to foreigners, she fought inside herself battling with the blue print of her existence and purpose in life, suddenly a moment of free thinking detached itself and broke free, her finger came down on the button and issued the ticket. Phew, bloody hell I thought I was going to get swallowed up again. I took it from her quickly whilst she was still dazed in case she changed her mind and without any delay went to locate a bus.

The one I needed was already here and being loaded up with peoples belongings. I followed with my eyes a curious trail of red that led to the rear of the bus and then into the open luggage compartment; there were three or four large sacks from which the red was dripping from, there I could see a large red stain around its nose, aaaaah pigs, I threw my rucksack on top and boarded my ride.

I was thinking about something, or was about to realise something, or I was . . . . I don't know, then as always something broke my train of thought and I glanced down at the time on my watch it read 1:21 and 21 seconds, 1st January, what are these moments in time that I get very often when my mind is free wheeling and suddenly for no reason it breaks off to notice the time, or the trip meter in the car, or the change from some shopping bill, these patterns, synchronisities and coincidences? There were strange vibrations in the air stirring in the depths of my soul as I tried to summarize the past events in my life leading me to this present moment. Somehow I was trying to conclude, summarize, and give form to something that wanted to remain formless, this journey, my inner questions, the decisions and outcomes of all these events. I could almost see it, like remembering a really interesting dream but something eluded me. I felt cheated, disappointed, an anti climax I suppose. Here I was after days of travelling through crazy, freezing terrain, all those strange faces and places, finally had I reached my goal? Was it here in Lhasa, what was next? When do we ever get to where we really want to be? Maybe I was already where I needed to be, that you do not need to climb a mountain to know how high it is.

It was New Years Eve I had reached the roof of the world and booked into another hotel for a night of luxury and a bloody good bit of personal hygiene. My thoughts come back to the present.

"Its not here." I thought.

No prize, no pot of gold at the end of the rainbow, no revelation, no enlightenment, just an unimpressive full stop!

I looked around the room and again the luxury of it all disappointed me, it was all too easy, too comfortable, soul-less, sterile and here I was in the belly button of the the world, and the Himalayas.

I drifted back to a few memories ago and it became Christmas again. I was in Chormas house after walking all that way to bring fresh vegetables, my mind became saturated again with the aroma and taste of simplicity, the communion between people, that was what I was missing, the richness of the simplicity, truthfulness and the subtle detail of the little bits in life that gives it all more substance and meaning.

I longed to be out of here walking amongst the small villages and the bamboo houses, banana tree blankets under a moon lit night and to be able to see through the cracks in the wall, hear the subtleness of the night lullaby me to sleep. Suddenly I hear a Tibetan song on the TV and my eyes fill up a little as I realize its the song I heard in Chormas house, strange coincidences again. I learnt that the title of the song was called 'Chorma' and that was where her name may have come from. It was just simply beautiful.

Here at the roof of the world and centre of Buddhist less is more faith, I am surrounded by luxurious hotels and TV adverts of more is more, there was nothing simple or humble here, it all felt wrong, out of place. I guess that's what the disappointment was.

I watched a speech on the TV representing the Chinese people, their ideals, their status, global issues, humanity I was not concerned whether it represented them truthfully politically in light of their occupation here, but it was a good speech valuing honour, respect, care, and community, things which seem a million miles away these days of fantastic plastic priorities, double glazed over with pride and ego. I wished for a better world, I wished for a really new year!

I drifted back to some very early memories of myself and growing up I suddenly remember the innocence of it all. I could actual feel it like remembering a certain taste or smell, that transcends thought and become experience. At this moment I was experiencing the innocence again and it was beautiful, truthful. I had nothing negative in my heart at all and slowly I could trace it forward in time through all the years until I found the first signs of its erosion.

I was always creative from very early on, enjoyed life and everything to do with it, enjoyed my health, sport, fitness, working with my hands and continued to enjoy all the arts through to my present time, to be creative was important and to express the world around me was impossible not to do. I could not ignore it, life I felt it was too huge, too interesting, too beautiful. I found and I discovered that I could do many things, it was like being able to connect to some cosmic energy, fuelled by the imagination where there were an infinite supply of ideas and enthusiasm on tap; whatever I put my hand to and whatever material I felt in my hands I could understand its structure, enjoy it and know how to work with it. I found I could create things, cooking, drawing, painting, photography, even mechanics there was a symmetry, performance and beauty to it all; the sweetness of the engine when everything starts working in harmony together was analogous to life. Life had a rich and varied palette of colours, textures, tastes, shapes and lines to be arranged, manipulated and explored.

Conversations I would get equally passionate about enjoying the beauty to explore deep into many subjects, there is so much to explore in this world, to think about and to discover. I started to realize how alone I was on this journey of discovery. I was sad that other people did not see the things the way I did; and then I saw that was my conflict creating divisions I made by judging and comparing, is a trap we all fall into. I thought they could not see it, did not want to, or found it tiring, and I thought they were missing out on so much, did they not have any passion for anything in life except the way they look and who they could convince to sleep with them, to make them feel good and loved, was that life a manipulation? Could they not apply themselves to anything more, something deeper? I never questioned it all until later when my innocence opened up to avenues of distrust, jealousy and conspiracy. Friends that I had once admired and put high upon pedestals suddenly tumbled and fell, faces became grey, suspicious and my world fell apart. Everything fragmented into an impossible puzzle where there is no point to it all, no super glue that will hold them back together again. Everything eventually changes though. I realized that life is change every second, nothing is ever static or stationary in nature, and that is the root of suffering to want something, wanting to keep it, knowing that whatever we have does not stay with us, our girlfriend, wife, our bank balance, our new things become old and break, and die, in this life all of it is impermanent, it is just borrowed for a moment, even our lives, we cannot keep it, it is just a temporary experience.

I had to go out there and find the person I once was. I have to find my faith again, my passion, because people, our culture, our politics, the bits of paper with demands for this and that chip away and wear away at your spirit, eventually leaving you with gaps and holes where doubt and fear seep into.

I guess I am an artist, that's my problem. I am romantic and believe in beautiful things. I see the infinite in all things, the imagination has no boundaries, no borders, passports or control there is no need, it's a beautiful world in here, no suspicion, no jealousy no greed, so much detail, so much colour, form and substance to it all, such interesting detail why cannot others not see it?

"He who see only a grain of sand in his hand sees himself only, he who see the infinite in all things sees God"
William Blake.

If the spirit is willing the flesh will follow, albeit sometimes very reluctantly!

I sit with my feet in a bowl of good warm water with eyes closed, becoming totally absorbed by this novel feeling, a sensation that I had forgotten and now rekindled. I traced the sensation in my mind, first by locating the source of it and followed the sensation of it with my mind as it permeated slowly from the extremities of my toes, then slowly penetrating within, eventually saturating the blood inside my veins in warmth. I feel the relief deep inside, something so simple as warmth, never really experienced before like this until after you have truly suffered, an inner warmth, of simple pleasure, just to be warm. It was amazing. I kept my eyes closed and simply became the sensation, the experience of warmth. Then I noticed a familiar smell, of road, dust, sweat, and grime, it was the steam rising up from the water which had dissolved small particles of the historic layers on my trousers, then into my nostrils, then my brain quickly categorised each chemical composition and put it in the relevant pigeon hole, experience and memory. Finally painting a pretty grim picture of trouser abuse in my mind. I open my eyes to take at look at myself and yes looking down at the state of my clothes the transformation was complete. I believe I had become Tibetan! My exposed skin was dirty with bits of black scales, that I had no idea where they came from but I saw the same sort of stains and dark patches on everyone else; my clothes were dusty, greasy, stained and my hair started to form small dreadlocks, yes this was a hard country, especially now in the winter nothing grew, no green, no fire wood to burn, they had to collect the dung from cattle and dry in the sun and use sparingly to cook and to keep warm, they wrapped themselves up in heavy cloth and fur to keep warm, food was basic. One Tibetan explained to me that it was upsetting for them as Buddhists because it was impossible for them to be vegetarian as they would prefer to honour their faith of not wanting to harm anything, but because conditions were so hard they only had yak meat to survive over the long winter, so had to compromise. Yes life was hard here.

The following day in Lhasa everything looked much better in daylight and especially after a good night rest. I walked all around and watched the many pilgrims that walked, prostrated, prayed, prostrated, prayed, prostrated, prayed and devoted themselves to their beliefs and ideals. They were as poor as hell I presumed, many must have travelled many hard miles to be here. I thought about all the others that must have dreamt to be here one day and here I was now just casually walking around for my own amusement. I felt a little guilty about this. I did appreciate being here though and promptly marched up to where the prayer flags were being sold and I joined the line of people that were walking towards a big lump of rock where all the flags, prayers, wishes were tied to blow free in the wind and be carried around the world forever. The idea of it was something beautiful to me whether you invest in this way of thinking or not, is not important but the symbolism is, it shows how these people can transcend beyond their poverty and hardships, this physical realm seems to be just a temporary inconvenience a stepping stone towards a better incarnation next time around. Some people ask me many times when I spend hours preparing food that will be eaten in just a few minutes, how can you do it? Why bother? I bother because I care about it, it is beautiful just to do something well, anything well and that beauty will pass on to others no matter how temporary it is.

My mother wrote to me once, she told me

"Everything that the heart gives away is never lost; it is kept in the hearts of others forever"

I liked that, do things because it a good thing to do and do not think of what you will get in return.

I smell the incense, and I am lost amongst the Tibetan chanting below . . ."Om mani padme hum . . . . Jewel in the Lotus of the Heart." That is where paradise is located, that is what we lost.

Smoke, incense, prayers, consciousness sailed away on the winds of hope, faith and freedom. There are many impossible places to reach in this world but here nothing could stop something as simple as this from going wherever it needed to. I hoped into every home and into every heart so they too could feel such simplicity, love and have time to listen, to care and to find paradise within.

With this I suddenly felt complete. I had said my own silent prayer, in my own way in fitting to all religions all over the world; that we are all the same, we all want the same thing at the end of the day, regardless of race, colour, religion, gender. We all need love, light and peace.

With this fresh in my heart I left, or rather floated over to enter the world of buses and bus tickets once again and to head to the border of Nepal. I became excited thinking about what was next . . . . to explore the heart of the Himalayas, the roof of the world . . . . Sagamartha, yes I am coming.

I Would Like
A Bus Ticket To Lhasa
Please...

Chapter 11

Inside the familiar cold grey walls of the bus ticket office I walked confidently up to the ticket booth, and peacefully demanded:

"I go Nepal, Pleeeeeeeeeeeeeease."

"No!"

Came back the familiar reply.

"What! No, no, no, no, look I have visa, its good, its good look at it . . . . and this . . . . look, yeah a travel permit, yeah . . . . Go on then tell me I can't go, I dare you."

"No!"

Came back the reply again.

She thrust my passport and bits of paper back at me through the slit in the window, eh! What is going on? I examine my permit that she was pointing to and waving around.

"What do you mean it's no good?"

She points to the date at the top that now read 2008/30/12 . . . . No . . . . It took a while for it to register in my mind, then in disbelief I saw that it was already out of date . . . . I couldn't believe it, they must have made a mistake and only gave me one day to get out of Tibet; they really did mean don't pass go, don't stop in Lhasa and go directly to Nepal, shit! I looked at the permit again trying to deny what my eyes were registering, shit . . . after all the hassle I went through to get it, again I carefully examined it in detail, but no matter how much I wanted to see otherwise, the blotchy red ink stamp remained out of date, and there was no mistake, it was definitely finally out of date. Then a surge of defiance swept over me and I suddenly felt an idea forming. I looked at the numbers again and make a few quick calculations using an old scrabble compartment of my mind; Hmmmmm . . . . aha, yes maybe with a little re-working, if I change the 8 and scratch off the lower half it will become a 9, then if I remove the 0 from the 30, then remove the 2 from the 12 it will become 2009/3 /1 . . . . ha haaaa! which means I still have two days left, ha haaaaaa . . . . I rushed off to find a sheltered place to start work on the forgery straight away. I found a sort of café and set about the great work; the bad quality printing was a great advantage and was easy to re work, so with a little smudging, scraping, creasing, adding a bit of road grime from my trousers and coughing on it for good luck, it looked perfect. I was impressed.

I returned to the station but funny enough they all seemed to recognized me! and again I got nowhere, they would not even engage in any kind of communication. I stood around trying to catch someone's attention and eventually a guy comes up who seemed curious with all the hassle I was having. I try to explain to him that I just want to go to Nepal. I point to the ticket booth and try to offer him money to buy a ticket for me, he shakes his head then pulls my arm to follow him, he leads me outside and shows me a bus and points to go inside, then holds his hand out for payment, hmmmm! I have no idea who he is but my options are running thin again. I decide to pay him the agreed amount, which was the hand sign equivalent to a few hundred Yuan, which seemed to be about right and what I expected to pay for the distance to travel, which was maybe 500 km to the border.

It all seemed a bit too easy and unorthodox, so nervously I waited on board to see what would happen next. All I could do was presume they knew where I wanted to go but I felt that they did not really understand me, that it was more important just to bundle you on to some sort of transport out of there, take some money from you and then you are out of their responsibility. I decided to try to get a second opinion and got out my now very crumpled torn map, selected an appropriate looking passenger and pointed to the border of Nepal, he took it from me, examined it from the front and the back, then upside down, back to front and then handed it to someone else who did the same, apart from amusing a few people and passing at little time whilst waiting for the bus to depart, nothing else happened and they handed it back to me and just smiled. I asked if this bus went here, pointing at the map again, again they just smiled so I smiled back, shrugged and waited for the bus to depart; another magical mystery tour no doubt. I started to think about the fare of a 100 Yuan which seemed a little cheap for a 500 km ride! My instincts were saying it's not over yet boy, you not out of here yet, 2 days left on my permit and I was getting very bored with bus stations and trying to get tickets. I really did not want any more problems now or have deal with formalities all over again, time was running out, no! It had ran out, we were on forged time and there were no more numbers left to re arrange.

6 hours later in the darkness of night, the bus drove into a large grey town, slowed down, indicated and pulled into a bay. Everybody got up and gathered their belongings. Well this looks like the end of the ride then I guessed. I tried to

ask where the hell we were, and pointed to my map again. Where ever we were I was sure it was not Nepal. They shook their heads and I had no choice but to face the freezing night and start to piece things together. I was somewhere between Lhasa and the border of Nepal, it was about 9.30pm, my mood felt as grey and cold as this place looked, no, recap it was bloody freezing cold.

I tried to pick an interesting direction that looked like it might have another bus station but it all looked grey and uninspiring. I started walking and asked a few locals for the bus station, and which there seemed to be one close by. I arrived there shortly around the next corner. I entered a grey concrete room that looked like the dole office in Brownhills, another grey place where I grew up in the Midlands and looked like the person behind the counter was as equally as depressed and unhelpful. I walked up to the familiar booth. I did not even try to appear cheerful, because I was not. I was so fed up with these buses deceiving me and falling short of my desired destination, giving me false hope, yes maybe that was the lesson don't expect anything, desire leads to disappointment, suffering! I could see her eyes which transcended the language barrier, her eyes were saying:

"Just don't bother asking, you are a foreigner, I should not even be looking at you."

She promptly returned my permit with a definite . . . . NO! attached to her mood.

What do they expect me to do then? Is this going to turn into 7 Years in Tibet!!! Am I destined to roam the deserted outposts of depressed bus terminals to the end of my days? Just let me get out of here.

Defeated and too deflated to be bothered with buses any more I looked around for somewhere to stay for the night, I found and booked into the first place available. The woman at the desk spoke a little English, very badly but enough to understand and to explain to me that no way was I going to get a ticket even with my travel permit. Foreigners are just not allowed to travel on their own through here regardless of what permit they have and there are severe consequences for anyone trying to help a foreigner to do so, this explains the fear and denial I had been encountering. Why this fear and this paranoia?

I lay in my room that night thinking about the distance, the time left and really not wanting to be captured and processed again; I was starting to feel like a cheap can of processed merchandise, with a gradually depleting sell by date that everyone was turning away from in disgust, well being captured once was enough and an interesting experience in the end, but now I just wanted out of here and on to new things. I started dreaming of mountains, nature, freedom to be walking unhindered, with my little guest house on my shoulders, yes I wanted to be free.

I go down to the woman on the desk again and try to ask something a little more complicated, like what can I do to get out of here, she seemed to understand and sympathise but could not reply. I decided to hang around and deliberately loitered about the lobby looking depressed and lonely until something happened, tactics which seemed to get results and I was impressed with my ingenuity, maybe she succumbed to these tactics or actually felt she wanted to help somehow, and finally she picked up the telephone dialled a number and passed me the phone. I answered and a man asked me in English what my trouble was. I explained that I was really fed up and about to start hitch hiking very soon to try to get to the border of Nepal before my permits run out in 24 hours. He asked me twice if I was sure I had all the correct papers, permits and visa,

"Yes, yes, sure no problem I have them."

" OK be ready at 5.OO am and a car will come for you, I have friends on their way now from Lhasa and are going to the border town."

Great this was amazing. I thanked him and the woman at the desk then went back to my room for a few hours sleep, relieved to be in transit again soon.

I was awake again before my alarm went off as always, then packed my bag and went down to wait for the ride. It was already an hour late and I was starting to get nervous again and preparing myself mentally to start hitch hiking, then suddenly a big 4by4 turned up. I excitedly gathered my things and opened the rear door to see that it was crammed full of Tibetans; it looked like a refugee run to the border. I squeezed in and looked around, everyone looked terrible like they have been driving for 48 hours over mountain passes, getting stuck, replacing flat tires and freezing half to death, just another normal day in Tibet I guess.

We ride maybe 2 hours out into the freezing dark morning into a huge high altitude wasteland, just as the sun was starting to appear above the horizon . . . . Pssssssssssst, bok bok bok bok bok bok . . . . we get a flat, I laugh and the whole process starts over again in my mind, maybe after we repair the tyre then there will be a fatal Yak collision, then a high mountain pass of impassable ice, maybe attacked by rabid snow leopards, check points and every conceivable obstacle the Gods decide to invent. I was preparing again for the impossible to happen. We all get out to lighten the load and stand around as the tyre gets changed. I look at my thermometer that is against my body and its hovering around—20 my hands and feet quickly get numb. I am thinking of Nepal and the mountains wondering what it will be like up there, with that thought I suddenly feel twice as cold and instead try to imagine tropical beaches, banana trees, sea water as hot as a bath. Hmmmm life is just an illusion, concentrate, warm warm warm!!!

Twenty minutes later wheels have been changed and we are on our way again. It was a hard, rough, dry, dusty road and I could see to my left, to the south an incredible horizon of white capped mountains, the Himalayas, someone pointed out the distant black familiar pyramid shape which was Everest, her head way up there in the clouds, the roof of the world and it really felt like it. My God this place was so vast, so huge, we were speeding across a huge wide plateau which climbed up to a maximum elevation of 5000 meters, two large wooden poles at the side of the road, draped in prayer flags that were thrashing around in the strong wind, marked the highest point of this highway. We all got out and I sighed with emotion at this dramatic landscape which peered at me with speculating eyes saying . . . .

"You are so tiny little human."

Yes I know . . . !

I walked quickly just a few meters to get some good photographs and found myself soon out of breath gasping, wow there's really no air here, my head started to spin a little so I finished recording the scene and went back inside.

Apart from one other little incident nothing else major happened, no bandits, meteorites, volcanoes, bolts of lightning, nothing really just except a near death slide on sheet ice whilst descending down a steep part of the road, with a huge cliff-hanger potential on one side, where the car continued to silently slide towards, gathering momentum as I pressed my non-existent foot brake hard into the foot well of the car, to no avail it kept bloody sliding closer to the end of the world; neither did the drivers frantic thrashing about on the real controls did any good either it just slid silently and gracefully towards a huge precipice that was getting closer and closer . . . . shhhhhhhhhit . . . . ptshhhhhhhhhhh . . . . thud . . . .

Just before we were about to see if there was indeed a God, we hit a very low concrete block which prevented anyone else's curiosity from exploring any further into this concept.

Bloody lucky again . . . . Once my blood pressure had settled down again I spent a little time thinking about this fatalistic philosophy. You know fate, when it's your time to go you will go and all the other times somehow you get away with it . . . ! Maybe! Well I was certainly starting to think that it was not yet my time; that I had much more to do, much more to see before I found that final exit and game over.

A little pushing later, shoving and straightening of body parts and the journey continued on its way, albeit very, very slowly this time, oh, and he decided to engage four wheel drive this time . . . . whoops . . . . eh!

We arrived at the border town, too late in the evening to go through but happy now that I was here and no one had to use a can opener to remove me from my final destination. I found a cheap room and settle down for the evening; yes tomorrow I will be in Nepal I rewarded my mind with that thought, different faces, sights, sounds and sensations.

Chinese Formalities
With Pink Pig Tails...

Chapter 12

I waited patiently whilst formalities multiplied like a lethal virus inside her head; she looked at my passport for an uncomfortable amount of time, without blinking or showing any signs of emotion. Flicking back and forward through the pages, maybe she was looking for her favourite part . . . . the bit that was missing, so that she could execute her next line of command . . . .

"Take him away to be tortured . . ."

She seemed to be getting flustered a little now between all the amounting entry and exit dates, border stamps that had taken a strong residency within my passport until she finally looked up at me frowning, she said in English: "Now remove your hat . . . . stand on one leg . . . . now whistle the Chinese national anthem, but do it backwards, and then . . . . make me smile!!!"

I smiled, these formalities were getting the better of my imagination, so I removed my hat instead.

She squinted accusingly at me and then started frantically waving a piece of paper at me, eeeeek . . . . I jumped back, a little threatened by her sudden outburst of stationary. This particular piece of paper had big, red, dangerous looking Chinese characters written all over it in important places and a big official looking stamp at the bottom. I was thinking maybe she had won the local ping pong competition and was very excited about her certificate she had won. My mind was getting more and more bored with all this official stuff, so it played with the scene a little more and stored parts of it in the travel compartment for future amusement, then it came back and started to pay attention again, aaaaah . . . . a thought occurred to me, obviously she wanted me to produce one of these from somewhere, out my bottom maybe! because unless I could suddenly become a magician, it would take a miracle to produce one of those. I must admit it did look lovely and official and I am sure if I had one of those I could travel where the hell I felt like for the rest of my time on earth, but I had not sold my soul and did not have one. I replied,

"Mee ho" . . . . No!

I had no idea what this thing was and as far as I was concerned I had everything I needed; I had my forged travel permit; my extended Chinese visa still valid woo hoo, old bus tickets, chewing gum, and plenty of black sticky stuff with bits of what looked like old Yak pubic hair. I was only trying to get out of their country not remain there! Then there followed a kind of Chinese verses foreigner stale mate whereby neither of us was budging from our position, she was locked in some kind of mind control from her superiors and I was just fumbling about hopelessly trying to give her what I couldn't, she continued to wave this piece of paper at me getting more and more excited about it all; I was worried that I was seriously in danger of getting a very bad paper cut if she got any closer.

I fumbled about deeper into my belongings and got together as much documentation as I could find, old bus tickets, crisp packets, sticky brown stuff from deep within the corner of my pocket and waved everything back at her in retaliation . . . . ha ha . . . . take that . . . . and this . . . . I waved bus tickets at her, note pads, receipts, maps, peanuts and another lump of sticky, furry stuff that I wish I had not found. Finally I shrugged my shoulders and smiled at her trying to soften her military lipstick and again desperately pleaded . . . .

"Mee ho"

I was hoping she would give up now and admit defeat, after all my collection of paper work was far more interest than hers, but no . . . . instead she looked at me hard in the eyes and said

"Wait"

She marched off military style to the corner of the room with a phone in her hand and proceeded to converse with her superiors; I think she was really pissed off and hoping to use torture on me next, ooh handcuffs whips . . . . Hmmmm some people would pay bloody good money for that!

She returned, looked at me for some time again obviously trying to decide what to do. Well by this time we had spent quite a bit of time together and I was starting to get to like her, a little excitable maybe, but I think it was the length of time that we had spent together, or was it was just my mind getting bored with the situation, which allowed the fantasy department of my mind to unlock the . . . . not so well locked door to the beautiful Asian woman archive . . . . I sniggered a little as I now saw her in pigtails surrounded by huge pink fluffy bunny rabbits, maybe this was her true form and she was not quite so hard after all, just a little cute, harmless, beautiful, Chinese woman who was still staring coldly into my soul, who just last week her husband had ran off with a more cute bunny rabbit and of whom I resembled very, very closely to . . . . aha..! that's why she was looking at me so closely with eyes that seemed to want to rip off my dangly bits, at my passport photo, telling me to remove my hat . . . . my disguise, yes that's it . . . . ! she thinks I am her run away, philandering bunny rabbit husband . . . ancient Chinese implements of torture, burnt deep in her soul wanting justice and revenge for crimes I did not commit. Yes it was that, I could see it, I was sure of it.

The rabbit was now making cute little bunny hops around the room, going eeek eeek eeeek, but her mouth was speaking something else that I could not hear. I tried not to snigger so coughed instead, the rabbit then suddenly disappeared and the one in the uniform was handing me back my passport, she pointed towards the exit obviously defeated . . . . and that was it, China was over! I felt a little sad to be leaving now it had been such a colourful experience, but over there on the other side of the friendship bridge lay Nepal.

I walked past two guards who were busy pushing an Indian man back to the Nepalese border, he was waving his bits of paper back at them, but they were more interested in pushing him about.

I love this instant change across borders, literally as you walk a few meters from one country to another it all changes, yet thinking about it all deeper I still find it weird that things are divided up this way.

I recognized the familiar smells of incense, betel nut stains, Nepali dialect, sights and sounds that were comforting, and food . . . . aah yes . . . . daal baat that makes you fart like nuclear waste discharge and also aloo, saag, roti, hot spicy acha . . . . yes I was looking forward to some good Nepali food.

I went through the visa processing quick and easy then jumped in a car to take me to Kathmandu I wasted no time there and quickly booked into a room and started the process of arranging a visa for India and a trekking permit for a little walk up to Everest base camp. I needed to wait for a few days for my Indian visa, which gave just enough time for pollution to build up once again in my lungs, to the point where I think just two more days here and I would be dead, after suffocating on the infected fluids of my own lung lining. I was desperately clinging on to health hoping to survive just a bit longer and then would be out of here. I cannot wait to get out the pollution was the worst I have come across. I took a little ride out to a temple that was high up looking down above the city, which became a sprawling mass of concrete blocks, as far as the eye can see and eventually disappearing, swallowed up in the distant soup like atmosphere, a 360 degree panoramic sea of noise, filth and fumes.

I planned to go to Jiri which is the starting point for trekking to Everest base camp, it follows the original route that the first explorers used on their attempts on Everest.

I feel lucky to have made it this far already and now this was bonus material, the 'grande finale' and then back home. I actually get to walk to Sagamartha I was excited, the roof of the world. I had spent quite some time in the Pyrenees last summer and winter which had re-kindled an old flame of mine from earlier times in England. I used to love getting out at the weekends and walking amongst nature, Yorkshire Dales, Lake District and many places in the dramatic landscapes of Wales. Now I was going to be in one of the most dramatic, highest places on earth.

I arranged my Indian visa prior to the walk so that on the return journey south from the base camp I hoped I could take a 4 or 5 day detour towards the south east, through some remote places and end up not too far away from the

Indian border, where from I hoped to find a Jeep, a bus, donkey, yak, to carry me to the border, and cross over into India where a good friend of mine was living not far away and was waiting for my arrival.

People that I had spoke to said it would take about three weeks to walk this route, but I needed to do it in much less time as I had no room on my Nepal visa for getting lost or tired, and certainly did not want any more trouble.

The last few days whilst waiting for my Visa I had tried to keep myself off the polluted streets and had taken some yoga lessons with the idea of getting a little more conditioned and supple than I was. My teacher was an Indian guy with bleached hair that had turned it a kind of ginger colour, it was hard to say how old he was as he had one of those ageless complexions that could have been anywhere between 33 and 103. He explained to me that the first day would be very simple exercises to cleanse and prepare the body for later on in the program. We went through some simple routines going over each part of the body, stretching, breathing, nothing that was meant to cause any discomfort, then we did a couple of exercises that he said would massage your internal organs, this involved pressing parts of your hands into your gut whilst letting out all your breath out slowly, crunching up into a fetal position until you were about to pass out. I think this was the one exercise that must have loosened something inside, because something definitely happened and I remember feeling really good immediately afterwards but later on that night some strange, terrible reaction occurred. I was producing the most incredible amount of gas, farting like crazy, it was legendary, far more than any daal baat that I had eaten or baked bean, strong beer and closing time kebab could ever produce, it was just not possible how much gas was being produced, and where it was all coming from? And why was I not deflating to the size of a ping pong ball? I started thinking that maybe the contractions of the exercise had produced a very tiny rupture from within my gut and had collapsed to form a small rift in the space time continuum, whereby volatile interstellar matter was now flooding into my intestines from the far reaches of the opposite side of the cosmos, albeit very stinky ones? I had not eaten anything that dangerous to explain it any other way.

It was amusing me at first like any childish bloke humour is, you know this juvenile sort of toilet humour that is to most men, very very funny for the duration of their immaturity and remainder of their adult life, but then it got beyond a joke even for me. I actually became disgusted and a little worried about myself, it just would not stop, in fact I could feel that the frequency and volume was building up to some sort of grand finale and was worried that there would not be a toilet big enough to deal with it. I could feel some sort of pre empty strike engage, and deep inside something started to gurgle in small familiar fluctuations, and then a barrage of detonators started systematically firing as though to induce an avalanche, then suddenly I felt it. It was like a small earthquake deep inside my gut. I froze, clenched slightly in desperation but instinctively knowing nothing was going to hold this back. I made a split second decision to sprint towards the toilet, somehow managing to remove the necessary clothes just in time to land my arse and firmly wedged it within the toilet bowl holding on for dear life . . . .

"Euston we have primary ignition, all systems are go for launch." What followed next was as though the entire contents and the lining of my intestines came out under high methane, rocket fuelled pressure . . . .

"Euston we have secondary burn, 3,2,1 . . . . Lift off"

BOOOOOOOM . . . .

"Jeeeeeeeeeeesus Christ." I claimed out loud and sat there for a while like a rabbit that had been momentarily caught in the headlamps of a large truck . . . . dazed, confused, shocked and very very empty, drained . . . . whatever it was . . . . it was definitely out now. I felt like a bloody big truck and had just ran over my soul and squeezed its contents out both material and non material. I shuddered. I felt like all the life force had just been jettisoned out of me and promptly crawled over to my bed to lay down. I tried to think if I had eaten anything unusual that could produce such a reaction and smell like Satan's private collection of inhuman toxic waste. I watched my old hiking socks shiver and cower away in disgust, retreating to a dark corner of the room, defeated that they now realised they were no longer the most toxic thing known to man.

All night became a relay race back and forward to that bloody toilet. I had already lost some weight from the weeks before and now I felt completely hollow, drained and weak.

I tried to take my mind off things and the smell, so drifted back to a few days ago when I met a guy from one of the many trekking agencies, who immediately pounced on me when I arrived, but seemed not too pushy, so I gave him my time. After going through a few things I let him arrange my trekking permits, my Indian visa, a cheap room for me, and obviously he was your best friend, so he invited and took me out to drink in his local part of the town to participate in a bit of a local 'Chang' and 'Tongba' bonding session. Tongba was a local brew, which I particularly became to like; it is brewed from millet and other 'secret' ingredients, jungle magic they tell me. The grain, millet is fermented then packed into a large wooden jug and hot water is then poured over to cover it, flavour and jungle magic seeps out from the fermented grain, which after a few minutes of steeping produces a mild, slightly alcoholic refreshing beverage, with I suspect maybe a trace of hallucinogenic additives and herbs that most witchdoctors and black magicians would not admit to using, but it's a good, long enjoyable drink which you can keep topping up with hot water producing a good brew, especially after a long days walk, the weak alcohol relaxes the muscles and the large quantity of water re-hydrates your body, so it's great, and I like to think that its medicinal, but you don't quite know if you are drunk or not or indeed tripping on the astral plane with delirium tremmon's in your brain, until you try to do something technical that is, like putting a key in a keyhole, you think you are perfectly normal until that final test at the end of the evening.

We drunk the Chang first which is some strange milky liquid of unknown origin, then the Tongba chaser followed then another one and a final one because I still felt perfectly normal, until kicking out time came and we went to meet his family and all sang and joked the night away and I eventually passed out. I woke in the morning wishing I had not:

"Oh no, not again."

I am in strange place, dark faces, children staring at me, uh! Where am? I . . . . what happened? Aha! yes you got drunk didn't you! Dam it! That Chang was strong this time, it had crept right up on me then . . . . wham! in the back of the head, "That's it." I prophesied no more of this stuff. I was wrestling with myself one side of me trying to be a yogi reaching dizzy heights of enlightenment, but instead I was fighting my western habits again, trying to reach new levels of alcohol abuse, yet nights like these were bloody good fun and hard to resist and seemed to break language barriers so well, or so I thought, not that you could remember.

I regularly went round to see him after that, at his work place and to talk and to drink chai and just pass the time away, he was an interesting, enthusiastic guy nothing too much trouble and loved to talk and to know everything about your world, this particular morning we changed from subject to subject and it became clear he was the man that could arrange anything, get anything, or if he couldn't his uncles, sister, brothers, sisters cousin could. Visas, souvenirs, transport, marriage, prostitutes, and 18 year old virgins . . . what . . . . ! I spat a little tea out by the casual way he went through his list of available merchandise and services, I looked back up at him, wiping the tea from my upper lip and draining the rest out of my nostrils, and I couldn't help notice that he had mysteriously transformed into Borat, the Kazakhstani character, dressed in a highly unfashionable bright blue suit, grinning wildly, looking very pleased with himself and speaking through a thick caterpillar moustache,

"Yeah sure, you know I get you a good a virgin from ma village, she a very good you know, and er vagin work a velly well, you have a great a sexy time with her, yeah."

I chuckled to myself, he really did look like Borat I had not noticed before but his suit, the moustache, yes it was Borat, ha!

"OK my friend then I find you a good English girlfriend in exchange, but I can't promise you any virgins though."

Hoping this would diffuse his train of thought and the impending marriage arrangements that I felt were sure to follow, but instead his eyes lit up and said:

"Ah yes, yes, we all have a good a sexy time, boom boom."

Oh God he got really excited now, so I humoured him a little more knowing that I really could not fulfil my side of the deal, and then suddenly Borat disappeared.

I walked around the streets of Kathmandu that night amused by the sprawling mass of people and narrow tall buildings, just a mass of visual detail and movement, sometimes your eyes did not know what they wanted to rest upon as there is simply too much going on. Music, bright lights, shops, restaurants and bars of course, buzzing, then suddenly nothing. The regular eight O clock power cut turned everything off, then slowly one by one, flickering yellow lights appeared like stars coming out at night, it was beautiful, such a transformation, mood and setting, a sudden transformation that revealed an underlying structure of calm. Instantly everything changed, there was a silence, no, there was a lot of noise but all the electrical noise had stopped and you could hear people living. I could hear the voices of people now which coincided with the puppetry of shadows that danced across the streets; in the corners of shops; windows projected elongated faces. Tonight was a spectacle of dance, light and shadow. Electricity and all its gadgets was such pollution it distracts us from seeing the simple things in life that are often really good and stimulating. I thought about this and it was true we have become so used to all this invasion of noise and disturbance, invisible noise also, the amount of wireless frequencies that must be flying around and cooking the softer more sensitive areas of our body and mind. No wonder we get headaches and cannot focus and concentrate, and why we feel so clear and uncluttered when we are on the top of a mountain or in the nature on long walks, by the ocean, there is just too much of everything and of things we cannot see.

I continue along the streets away from the main tourist areas into tiny back streets, dark faces everywhere peering back at me, and imagined doing this back in Manchester or one of a thousand built up inner city areas back in the so called civilized world, where there really would be a risk of being shot, mugged or beaten up just for the fun of it. I never feel threatened here, there does not seem to be same kind of attitude or crime in the hearts of these people, sure there is crime, theft that poverty fuels, but the attitude is different they would all prefer to work than to steal, and my God do they work hard and long hours for almost nothing, if they get to feed themselves they are doing well, they all seem so together, maybe it's something to do with their beliefs, that they do believe in something bigger than themselves that this is only temporary and to just do the best you can. I like these people. I love Asia.

There are many street children here, lots of begging, targeting the huge influx of foreign tourists heading out into the mountains. Sometimes it does get very tiring having to keep saying no, even just not saying anything at all is draining. Today I quickly dismissed a young lad that was tugging on my arm waving bits of paper at me, unfortunately he struck a sore spot there and I lost my cool.

"Oh no, not this again"

But there were no Chinese bureaucracy here hiding behind these bits of paper. I was hot, tired and a little short tempered so I had snapped at him to leave me alone and away he fled, but then I saw in my minds eye a glimpse of what was on the paper and what he was obviously trying to sell me. I suddenly felt guilty with my short temper, as I recollected a childlike drawing of Buddha. This young street lad maybe 8 had been drawing pictures on bits of crumpled paper that he must have found, of Buddha and other popular things that tourists might buy, maybe by copying things he had seen being sold in the shops, he thought he could make an honest rupee or two, in fact he had the initiative to start his own little business enterprise, he had cut out the middle man and produced a healthy pile of these drawings, instead of begging he was genuinely trying to do something, anything he could, to earn an honest rupee, wow . . . ! I realized this and I looked around for him to buy one or two of them but he was gone. I was too quick to judge, but I certainly hope his talents and determination have provided for him by now.

Jiri To Everest Base Camp

Chapter 13

Jiri—Everest base camp—Day 1

After spending too long in the frantic maze of people, pollution and chaos of Kathmandu. I was finally on my way to breathe the cleaner air of the Himalayas.

I had received my Indian visa and got out of there as fast as possible; my lungs actually ached and I started to hack and cough along with the dawn chorus of everyone else in this place. I felt sorry for these people having to live here grasping on to some thin thread of hope that a tourist tsunami would come along and liberate them all, it won't, the more they get, the more they want, the bigger it all gets, the bigger it expands, the harder it is to look after it all and it all suffocates itself in a dense cloud of fumes and phlegm. They are better off going back to the jungles farming and providing what they need from the natural resources around them.

It seems to be the less people have the more they want to share the little they have. The more people have, the more they fear losing it and less they want to share.

After a long bus ride we arrived in Jiri, to be immediately pounced upon by hopeful hotel and guest house owners. All

208

friendly enough but really did not understand that I wanted to get walking straight away, as it was getting late in the afternoon, with about three to four hours of light left. With that in mind I quickly marched out of there to find the start of the trail, which started at the far end of the market. I felt instantly relieved to be following a trail now that would take me away for many days of freedom and to be in the arms of mother nature again, just me and her. I was also happy to see that they had not developed any Mc Donalds and pizza huts here yet, which I had feared and had mentally prepared myself for this western invasion. I was not sure of how much development had affected this area. Most people fly from Kathmandu to Lukla, which is much higher up and much closer to the big mountains, so here was relatively unpopular and quiet. It would be a good week of walking and a good chance to acclimatize more as it slowly became more elevated.

I finished the day feeling very lazy. I had only walked a few hours but I felt it already, my body was wanting to slow down and it was complaining, resisting, stomach also was in dispute complaining that it was not getting fed enough, and my lungs still ached and felt like it had half the capacity than what it should have. I guess I was still weak from the big nuclear clear out, so I allowed for that and came to rest just as the light started to fade. There was a beautiful red sky that evening, with a biting chill in the air as the sun sank lower. I set up my tent up and called it a day, just 1km from Kinja.

KInja—Junbesi 9 hours—Day 2

A long hard climb this morning starting from 1650m up to 3550m nearly 2000m climb, five and a half hour slog to finally level out then following a contour to a pass at 3550m, then a long descent down into Junbesi, where the up muscles were given a rest but the sleeping down muscles got rudely woken up.

The way from Jiri was from west to east which meant crossing many rivers that flowed down from the Himalayas, which meant having to climbing in and out of many valleys, it was going to be a strenuous route. Darkness finally closing again as I turned the final corner to head north. There was a small village below me with a large monastery overlooking the valley and was extremely atmospheric. I made camp at this special vantage point and set my tent up in a good position for the sun to come and wake me up in the early morning. I walked over to a source of crystal clear, fresh Himalayan water and filled my bottle up thinking of all the rows of this stuff in the supermarkets with their marketing sales pitch, 'hand picked by Tibetan Llamas high up in the purity of the Himalayas' well I was no Llama but I was actually hand picking my own Himalayan water that evening and felt so fresh.

I stop to drink tea and eat biscuits in one of the little shacks along the way and it is starting to become unthinkable, what use to be a simple pleasure to be able to sit, re-cooperate a little and drink a few cups of good Chai is getting too expensive, they are seriously exploiting the high traffic of tourism here, money, greed, the spirit of things get lost and perverted. The children now are becoming more and more intrusive, where instead of being able to have a laugh and joke with them they have only one thing on their minds, rupee, rupee, bon, bon. We have created an image for them of walking wallets and gifts, what a shame to have this barrier.

Junbesi—Jubhing 9 hours—Day 3

Today was the first sighting of the big boys. Just after climbing 2 hours I turned a corner to head northwards to be greeted with a crystal clear view of the jagged Himalayan backdrop, Everest, Mira and some other smaller peaks (6000m 7000m hardly small) but certainly dwarfed by its towering neighbours, it had a surreal appearance to it all, so clear and so big words are too restrictive to give it justice, but it was like some well painted theatre backdrop, unreal but I felt as though I could just reach out and touch it all.

There was such a noticeable difference in temperature now as I were mainly above 3500m the sun by day was strong and kept you very warm but as soon as it dipped behind one of the many rocky obstacles, it quickly dropped to well below freezing.

Jubhing—Lukla 10 hours Day 4

It was a hard day today I had not slept well because of a sneezing fit all night and battling with mopping up torrents of snot everywhere, looks like I had caught a chill which had developed into a streaming cold, so it was a heavy start to the day with another long 2000m climb up a steep trail, 5 hours of stumbling on the loose rocky surface with this and snot constantly cascading down my face I was finding it very hard, but not as hard as the many locals I saw along the way, a long line of ant like characters, ferrying supplies up and down this bloody long climb. They were carrying huge loads on their backs, many of which I just could not believe what they were carrying. I will never complain again how heavy my rucksack is. I tried to do a quick calculation of maybe 120 kilos, one had nine 1 gallon containers of oil, plus a large crate of beer, noodles and everything else that could be possibly tied strapped or hung off his wicker basket, a strap went around and up over his head so that the weight will be on his head and neck, I could not imagine lifting this let alone walking up what I had just struggled to get up with my 18 kilos with modern equipment.

I found a place to set camp and this day it was is a relief to stop, a bit short of where I had hoped to reach at Lukla, but I think not far from here, there is a market on in the morning and I hope to pick up some food supplies.

Lukla—Namche Bazaar 9 hours Day 5

Another long tiring day my system is still at a low with this dam cold and I am getting frustrated as I can feel it is holding me back. I want to feel good again and enjoy the walking rather than it being a battle of determination.

From here things suddenly changed I saw many hotels, guest houses, and even bars to meet the demands of all the tourists that must fly here into Lukla.

Namchee Bazaar—Orsho 8 hours Day 6

Again a hard climb, seems to be no where that is flat in Nepal, at around 4.00pm I decide to stop early and rest up, I had nothing left any more to give. I was starting to feel the altitude a little which seemed to add a few extra kilos to every step. I was happy with the progress though, just 2 days now and I should be at the base camp. I hoped my energy would be fully restored soon.

Orsho—Lobuche 7 hours Day 7

Another bad night sleep for some reason I had a bad stomach again and had to keep dashing outside, which you really do not like to do when you are nice and warm inside a sleeping bag, having to unzip and brave the sub zero temperature outside to drop a crap, this I really did not need and I woke in the morning feeling completely drained and pale.

I took it easy for the rest of the day, and settled down into a very slow pace, which became very enjoyable and I felt a new surge of life coming back. I felt so light inside, obviously from all the gastric problems from Kathmandu, my body already flushed out, eating very light food since then and also last night another big 'clear out' I felt surprisingly good though, just a little tiredness from not enough sleep but physically I felt different, light, good. I enjoyed the days walk, the trail climbed steadily up and became more dusty, desolate and definitely colder. I arrived at Lobuche 3.00pm it looked like a forgotten outpost of corrugated tin and wooden huts, so I found a quiet spot to set up my tent. It became very windy and suddenly a blast came out of nowhere sending a cloud of fine dust into my tent, into my noodles that I was cooking, into my sleeping bag, my eyes, nostrils. I couldn't believe it, the mess was instant and incredible, it was like a mini tornado inside my tent had forced its way in, and promptly slapped me around the face a little then left just as quickly as it started. I sat there in disbelief, disgusted, everything covered in a heavy layer of dark grey dust. I took everything outside cleaned it all and then returned it, listening and waiting for another surprise attack. I tried to block up all the holes I could, when suddenly again it blasted my tent. I tried to pin myself up against the vents and holes with feet, hands, head, ass, anything I could but fine dust just came flooding in again from somewhere else, this time all I could do was to let it win, yes mother nature I know you are there but you don't have to keep reminding me though. Now suddenly it was silent again, nothing not a breath of wind she said what she wanted to and left. Weird!

I feel much better now, acclimatized at nearly 5000m I feel twice as good as what I did in China at the same height, no dizziness, no headaches, but still hard work and no accounting for the 50 percent shortage of oxygen in the air.

I reach my destination tomorrow, I will leave my tent here already set up to save as much weight as I can, it will be so enjoyable for once not having so much to carry.

The many prayer flags and Chortens I see all along this way all serve to appease the spirits and the mountains so as to grant the Sherpas safe passage. The flags are printed with holy Buddhist invocations:

Chapter 14

Om mani padmi hum

There is not a single aspect of the eighty-four thousand sections of the Buddha's teachings which is not contained in this six syllable mantra so translation is impossible into western language and thinking, but for visualization purposes it is described as 'The jewel in the lotus'

Purifies, Samsaric Realm. *Om,* bliss / pride, gods. *Ma,* jealousy / lust for entertainment, jealous gods. *Ni,* passion / desire, human. *Pe,* stupidity / prejudice, animal. *Me,* poverty / possessiveness, hungry ghost. *Hung,* aggression / hatred, hell . . .

Often there is a winged horse printed on the flags which are sacred creatures to the Sherpa's and are believed to carry the prayers heavenly with great speed. The Sherpa term for prayer flags is 'lung ta' which means winged horse.

Labouche—Kallar Pattar Day 8

-8 inside my tent this morning and my watch reads 6.30 I quickly get up to put on my layers before I get too cold, a blast of icy air takes my breath away as I unzip myself out into the world once more, but it was a different sort of cold that I have experienced anywhere else, a very dry cold, there was no moisture in the air at all and your lips cracked very easily, you can understand now the leathery complexion to all these Tibetans and Nepalese.

It was a joy to walk today with a light bag and all my bodily functions behaving themselves at last, it felt as though the closer I was getting to my goal the better I was feeling and I was, there was a definite spring in my step today although we were still high at over 5000m and still climbing. I had been catching up with and overtaking lots of other people who we all looking a bit worse for wear, doubled over at times, or flat on their backs on the floor rasping at the thin air, one was even carrying a big red medical pack from one of the local altitude sickness centers; this was the trouble of so many people who had flown into Lukla from 1000m straight up to 4000m then tried to walk up to the base camp at 5400m, without any acclimatization. Things were sure to get uncomfortable. I bounced along past them happily, thinking yes you get out of life what you are prepared put into life.

The trail eventually reached the edge of a huge glacier the Kumba valley and the trail snaked through large imposing boulders for about an hour to finally reach Gorak Shep, the last outpost before base camp, which was another jumble of shacks and a couple of corrugated restaurants . . . . ! I walked straight past over the helicopter pad and then started to climb Kalar Pattar at 9.00am, which is a little peak and boasts a great view of Everest.

It was a steep climb and I could feel the atmosphere was getting thinner and thinner by the step, cold, crisp air bit at the inside of my throat as I gasped for air. I could not keep up a continuous rhythm no matter how slow I tried to walk, after about every twelve paces it left me gasping again, with this process it took nearly 2 hours to finally reach the top. I resisted to turn around to look until I was right at the top as I wanted full impact of the elevation and vantage point to which the best view of Everest could be seen.

Finally all things eventually reach their summit. I was there. I stopped, rasped at the air again until I felt relaxed enough, then slowly turned around. The sky was completely blue not one cloud to be seen. I gazed speechless at the huge expanse of rugged terrain around me, it was hard to judge just how big this place was but I knew and I felt very, very small indeed. Then I saw her, a dark black pyramid piercing the upper stratosphere, Sagamartha, there you are, you are indeed very, very beautiful. I looked at her with respect and awe and she looked back at me to say "You silly little man, you so tiny" I thanked her anyway just to be here at the roof of the world and to have been given the strength and safe passage so far to be here, it was a truly a beautiful moment that I hold deep in my soul forever. I stood there a while longer trying to comprehend all the history of this place, this mountain, all the attempts to climb her nearly another 4000m higher and people have done it without the aid of oxygen,—70 below, old heavy equipment it was beyond my comprehension.

That was it, my journey had literally reached its peak. I got to the highest place I could. I paid my respects to Sagamartha and headed back to my little base camp. I reflected upon my journey so far. All those weeks ago starting from Thailand, the warmth of their smiles and the heat of the fresh chilies seemed far, far away in the past where it had all started from, sitting on that train waiting for it all to start. The land of smiles then on into Laos, full of innocence and simple life to cross over into China, strange signs that I could not read and even stranger orange chickens, then Shangri La, Chormas smiles, humble Christmas pie with stables and donkeys under a starry, starry night. Off on the forbidden road, crazy Frank Zappa death ride to freezing oblivion, shit! there I was thought I was going to die many times,—20 frosty testicles, I got no ticket to ride but I'm going to go anyway, got busted by Mr. Plod a paper chase of hell out of Tibet, get out don't pass go and go directly to Nepal, paid my dues, lost my face but paid my respects in Lhasa, where I tied my flags and tied my vows to leave freedom an ideology blowing in the wind. Nepali Thali, curry and spice made me empty deep inside. I got nothing left now so I went to climb the biggest mountain I could find, Sagamartha, Everest she was so kind and I felt a piece of love that would always stay inside.

All these memories all these places, faces, sights, sounds, sensations I have a huge palette now to play with for the rest of my days, a truly amazing world. Yet we are all travellers at the end of the day all navigating and trying to make the right decisions, choices and change of direction, sailing upon the surface of a rich tapestry upon the blue prints of life.

Labouche—Namchee Bazaar Day 9

It was a very cold night again—15 inside my tent so was very happy to quickly be on my way and walking to generate some body heat. Within a short time I warmed up and found myself flying along, wow! I am a walking machine, tak, tak, tak, tak, the more I descended the stronger I felt. My body must have got well acclimatized and now I feel as though I have twice as many resources at hand. I march along at full speed, enjoying the way my body is feeling and watching the scenery drift past. I plough up the hills like I have nitrous oxide fitted to my thighs and do not want to stop for anything. I am enjoying the ride so much, the rapidly changing scenery and looking forward to explore new places. My breathing is like I am at rest and my feet are in perfect rhythm, time flows by very easily along with the kilometres. I am somewhere else not really aware like in a dream my body is doing everything automatically whilst my mind feels completely free. I have a great sense of love welling up in my heart, of nature of beautiful things, feelings. I trace the sunlight as it filters, ray-tracing through the Himalayan foliage around me, it all seems so enhanced, bright, sparkly, clear, crystal clear like my mind is feeling and my heart. I feel very clean. I start to see lots of detail around me, colours, and shapes, patterns that have always been there but not truly observed or noticed. Nature is truly infinite. Never static always changing, we are no different we are also organic and abide to the same rules and changes, birth, death, rebirth. Matter cannot be completely destroyed or created it just changes from one state to another. We fear change, we get too precious about things, yet change is for sure, it is so important to accept change, nothing is ever permanent.

Mountains are a place of purity, exposed, we present ourselves, vulnerable, we are naked to the raw elements that can come down upon us, we have to be humble and respectful to survive. Mountains are a window to the soul and a union between man and nature and of our creator.

Namchee Bazaar—Kharikola 12 hours Day 10

I tried to write something in my diary today but I was completely spent, too tired after walking 12 hours late into the evening trying to get to Kharikola. Arrived 8.30, dark and set up tent. I collapsed into a deep sleep.

Kharikola—Nanjing 9 hours Day 11

From here now onwards we leave the main Base camp trail and head south east towards the Indian border, passing close by to Mira peak.

Another big start to the day turning off from the main trail on to a tiny trail that cut steeply up through a few houses and then to lose itself amongst heavy forest, which was difficult to follow but felt good to be within a more natural setting rather than all the rows of guest houses that had been prior to this. The trail finally levelled out and reached a small village in time as my stomach was complaining about food again. I had been strict with it for most of the week surviving on rations that I had prepared, dried food, pasta, and therefore I had lost a lot of weight. I could feel bone now when I sat down, it was uncomfortable, there was no padding on my rear any more, my arms were lean and I could see every muscle, but I felt really good better than I could ever remember.

I noticed a place where villagers were all eating, it looked good, bloody smelled good too, my stomach agreed and said what the hell are you waiting for, so I decided it was time to try to stock up with some extra calories. I dropped my bag to the floor outside where many curious faces were all watching me.

"Namaste, mira Kana . . . daal baat?"

"Hello can I come and eat some Daal Baat?" Someone points to sit down inside, so I go in and my eyes squint adjusting to the dark, smoky interior. I love it, the familiar smell of wood, cooking, spices and all the other condiments of Nepali lifestyle. Shafts of bright sunshine pierce through the bamboo slits in the wall, creating a 3 dimensional Venetian blind effect, as it illuminates and slices through the fog from the open fire. I sit and amuse myself for a while watching dragons and demons dance and fight with each other, this laser show of light, smoke and fire.

The food arrives, a huge plateful of rice, daal curry, a few curried potatoes and saag, spinach. Aaaaah yes I cannot wait to get into that, my stomach cannot wait, my eyes are bulging and mouth salivating. I dive in local style with my hand and scoop up a huge handful and pack it into my mouth, it's like I have been on a desert island for years the spices and different textures flood into and overwhelm my senses. I am very happy and I smile at the others

"ram ro cha, mito"

Very good, very tasty, they laugh, smile and the feeding continued. I finish and they fill my plate up again two more huge platefuls and I easily get it down, my stomach is swimming around in food bliss and is completely ecstatic, for a few more hours at least.

Fuelled up now and ready to go. I can see the way ahead from here, at the far end of the village the trail starts climbing up steeply again to a pass through and over a high ridge, and I guess it's going to use up at least half a plateful of Daal baat to get up there I calculate.

800 meters up, 2 hours later, hot and sweaty now with the midday sun, I turn to see the tiny houses of the village below where I came from and the thin streaks of kitchen smoke lazily drifting across the Himalayan range, aaahhh Daal baat, goodbye.

Now as I reach the top of the pass I can see for the first time the land to the east, a formidable horizon of mountains, rivers, and deep valleys. I can see the direction I need to go and it's not going to be easy, about three big rivers to cross which means three big climbs and descents as we traverse south east across them.

The trail descends now to the first river, it's unbelievable steep, and I have to grab hold of small shrubs and trees to lower myself down, for a very long way and my calf muscles feel like swollen balloons about to pop, but I am loving this part of Nepal, no guest houses, jungle, lots of it, a few tiny villages, I feel good here.

I enjoyed going to the base camp but the commercial squeeze is too much for me, it is good that they are earning a living but I think Sagamartha is holding her head in shame with this highway of chocolate wrappers to the top of the world.

It's a crazy descent to the river I am slipping on the dusty lose surface half climbing, hanging on to trees, peering down over a deep precipice into a raging river far below. I cross a long suspension bridge and take some video of this dramatic area, the noise of the river below drowning out any other sound. I am being looked down upon by two huge walls of rock and jungle either side of me, I feel so small again.

I start to climb up the other side it feels such a waste of energy I have just come all this way down to have to start climbing up again and then to do it all over again maybe another two times. I try not to think about it too much and drop down into slow pace.

I pass by a few tiny houses perched high up on the side of the mountain just unbelievable where some of these people are living, why the hell choose such a ridiculous location where many birds would even suffer with vertigo. I stop to talk and refresh myself with some of their water, these were the real local Nepali people, they were amazing, so friendly, curious, helpful, not wanting anything from you here and perfectly happy for you to stay, talk a little and just be.

I climb almost to the top, but I could feel the energy just starting to fade, then I notice a stone shelter built next to a stream in the middle of this forest, yes a perfect place to stay for the night I decide. I clear the ground, collected some wood for the night and arranged my things, so good to be outside like this. Soon my fire crackles away and I am warm, fed and completely relaxed, satisfied, complete, just enjoying the simplicity of this forest, listening to it's different sounds and sensations, it is so peaceful here, so quiet. I feel cradled in its arms and by the warmth and light of the fire. I settle down to a deep sleep.

Nanjing—Sonam Day 12

This was the biggest day so far with a 2000m climb then to drop down again another 1500m, both my up and down muscles were completely spent. I cannot believe how un-flat this place is, there was no relief from the relief at all, having to constantly stand on some sort of steep gradient and loose rock that was like trying to walk over a demolition site, my knees were sore and throbbing from the barrage of shock they were trying to absorb.

T the end of the day I came across a basic guest house, the first one I have seen on this trail and just before the next big pass. I see no good place to camp and feel the need of a good meal again, my body reserves are low. I had been dreaming about food the last few nights even my stomach comes to haunt me in my dream state. I was lost in some sort of junk food fantasy, enjoying this virtual treat of food fantasies, pizzas dripping with grease, chocolate, sandwiches of cream, honey, biscuit, caramel . . . . arrrgh I woke up sweating virtual sugar, fat and still grinding my teeth, and became very disappointed with the serious lack of sweet things that this waking reality presented. I laughed to myself whilst waiting for my next plate of food to arrive, aaaah yes we are going to feed well tonight as I suddenly catch a glimpse of what must have been either a very rare and precious, or an emergency jar of jam because it was locked away in a glass cabinet, and was trying to hide and conceal itself behind a bottle of pickles, this one thinks he is safely locked away. An idea leapt to mind . . . . Hmmmmmm pancakes. I am only small weighing in at this time what felt like probably 47kilos yet I have an uncontrollable appetite at times which is also fuelled by my passion for cooking and eating. At this moment I feel I can easily eat three times my own body weight. With a bit of creative sign language and getting a back stage pass to the kitchens, I managed to find flour and eggs and they quickly got into the the production of pancakes, then having struck up a suitably extortionate financial deal for the jar of special reserve jam, which I think I was prepared to pay in instalments for the next ten years for, the feast soon started and continued until I could no longer entertain anything to do with food. I belched and crawled on my hands and knees to my room, "No, leave me alone I'm full I've had enough,"

"aaah but sir its only wafer thin"

Tomorrow I will need all this fuel, the last big obstacle a 3400m pass. I was glad to have pushed hard yesterday to leave a short climb in the morning, after here things should get a little easier as we descend down into a valley to follow a river to Tumblingta, here I was hoping to find some sort of transport to get me to the border of India.

Sonam—Gothe Bazaar 8 hours Day 13

Very pleased with the progress it looks like I will complete the journey 1 week less than what was suggested, without compromising on missing out on any of the atmosphere.

I really enjoyed the guest house last night it was not like the others I had seen trying to compete with each other and providing all the European comforts they could. I come here to get away from our life style, to see something else, so I really enjoyed the basics here living as they do, we had no electricity, nothing, basic food, no menu just eat whatever they have available and are prepared to cook that evening, it's simple, its uncomplicated and leaves nothing to be disappointed about. I really feel like I am in real Nepal here.

Sonam—Gothe Bazaar 8 hours Day 14

I am still feeling great my body is well fed now and I am very light not carrying any excess. I enjoyed a long walk down to the valley below, crossing a suspension bridge and followed local trails through small villages; here I am lost in a timeless world of village life and crops that are being gathered.

I have just finished reading a book about the early attempts on Everest. I thought it topical but not something that proved to keep me feeling warm at night I must confess. There was an extract that I felt was very interesting it was written by a young Sherpa lad who had lost both parents to the commercialization of Everest, in fact all his family and relatives had died in the end trying to help rich foreigners who had no or very little experience to climb Everest, fuelled by their poverty they committed themselves into trying to assist these unworthy, money cushioned attempts to get these people to the top. Putting the lives of many Sherpas at risk and who consequentially died, his final statement was that Sagamartha is a sacred place and should only be reached by those worthy and able bodied people, and without the aid of oxygen that today still litters the side of something pure. It is mans desire and greed to fulfil egotistical goals at the expense of others and of the surrounding natural beauty it should be kept pure as possible.

It was a great day full of small villages and jungle scenery, no tourists and no guest houses. I feel that I want to walk forever now, never stop just keep going.

I walk late into the evening accompanied by a fantastic sunset behind me. I feel like some movie star in an exotic setting my shadow taller than my soul, stretching far out in front of me. I cross a small bridge and just as I was passing two bamboo houses, I stopped to watch an old woman, she was busy weaving some dried straw to form circle pads which she then bound together to make a comfortable little stool. I smiled but could not communicate apart from saying 'very good' in Nepali, she pointed to the house and made a sign to sleep with her hands, "Ok yeah great." I say, it did not take much convincing for me to stay here, I felt very at home. I had a great evening whereby her children and relatives came round to enjoy a new face and we all ate together and talked, laughed, joked. I really love these people.

I passed a similar place the day before, so peaceful I almost had to stop, but I felt if I did I would get stuck and never come back again. I would forget everything of the west and live this life with them. Their children were playing in the next field of freshly cut straw, all ages playing perfectly well, no crying, bullying or being spiteful. The relatives close by all busy with daily life, collecting, drying, making things, it was like you could feel the natural clockwork of the time, the season, the hour and everyone had their thing to do, it was beautiful, you could feel the love and warmth between them all, unhindered by clutter, free to apply care and attention all aspects of living as a unit, a village, a community. I know I am not one of them and never can be; but I see so much of what they have that other apparently more civilized cultures have lost.

Gothe Bazaar—Chainpur 6 hours Day15

I followed the local trails as best I could in the direction of the river that would soon intersect with the bigger ones that were running South. several times I got lost amongst the maze of small local trails and villages that started off in the right direction but then soon ended up inside someone's pig shed or front room, it was like that and I amused myself for most of the day this way to finally descend to the valley below at a heavily oxygen enriched altitude of 700m. I felt very, very fit.

I joined with the big river that was now like walking on the west coast of France, kilometres of almost white sand lined its dry river banks. I followed to finally arrive at Chainpur at around 2.00pm, a relatively small town/village but seemed like a sprawling chaotic mess again compared to the few days of jungle and simplicity. I mooched around for a while looking out for signs of transport. I came across a land rover packed full of locals and they agree to let me ride. I scrambled up on to the only available seat left, up on the roof, next to two others, a sack of oranges, potatoes, chickens, rice. I make friends with the sack of potatoes first and then wedged myself in for what was to be a very bumpy ride. The road was really rough, if you could call it a road that had to literally go through two rivers and then a camel trophy ride to arrive at Chainpur for 5.00pm.

I set up base camp literally in the bus station that night, which was a patch of dirt high up overlooking the southern Nepalese landscape, so that I would not miss any ride out of here early in the morning, thinking they would have to run me over first as I was told a bus may or may not arrive at 5.00 am maybe . . . . so I really did not want to miss it.

Chainpur—God knows where

First gear bus ride of hell. We set off down a road . . . ! Well I did see a sign that said this was a Nepalese development road, but I don't think this road had even been proposed, let alone developed in any way or even should have been driven on. I was not sure if I wanted to hand the bus driver a medal or sentence him for crimes committed against the gearbox and cruelty to buses in general. No matter how beat up or how old they were, they did not deserve this sort of abuse, to cross rivers, span crevasses, to defy motor mechanics and to supersede all the maximum tolerance specifications of its original design. The tortured engine screamed and continued to scream along in first gear for most of the journey, sometimes managing to get a pleasant crunch out of second or was it two and a half! All this and having to try to find some part of my arse that did have a little flesh remaining on it to cushion me from the hard seat and hammering ride. I had lost a lot of weight; I did not have too much to spare in the first place, and now it was painful to sit, my hair was matted, my face covered in a thick Chris Bonnington type mountaineering beard, dried snot, mud, dust, the cloth of my trousers were hiding behind a film of sweat, jungle and food that somehow missed my mouth. I looked a mess.

We crossed another river, literally straight through it, yes in a bus, it screamed across still in first, trying to keep up speed so as not to get stuck and bounced so high I left my seat and hit my head on the roof, nearly landing on the lap of the guy next to me. Then it climbed up the other side to come to a complete stop behind a collection of queuing vehicles. There were many people buzzing around, police, goats, and chickens which were all looking serious and pecking at the up turned truck in the middle of the road. Nothing was moving very much, or had been for some time it seemed. I got the story a little later that a child had been killed in a road accident, so emotions were very high, plenty of pointing and waving of arms around, crying, old men chewing betel, old women chewing betel, cats, dogs and the uncles brothers sisters cousin. Hours passed. I could not understand why things were not moving, there seemed to be enough room to go around, but by the look on everyone's faces they had all resigned to a long wait for some reason. Eventually the police decided they had enough Daal Baat and chai, cigarettes and made some sort of announcement, then out came those bits of paper again which got passed around and waved about at each other, this seems to be a reoccurring trend these days. Then more standing around. What is going on? Maybe they were waiting around until the soul had time to depart properly, sometime around 2.30 I hoped. Then there was a need for lots of shouting and more finger pointing, crying, then a protest. This became a cycle of events that went around at least four times in short emotional waves before they all started to get bored with it, the chickens left first, then the goats, then finally the people. Maybe they had got everything out of their system by now and any stray souls looking for the light had decided they were better of out of there. Their absence felt, the crowds dispersed along with them. Gingerly the vehicles went on by and for the next 8 hours I fidgeted uncomfortably on my bony ass as we crawled along in first again.

We arrived late because of the earlier morning hold up and had to stop short of our destination at a convenient town. I had no Nepalese currency on me now as the prices in the national parks broke my budget and there were no where to change any, so now it was late, dark, and I was tired with no enthusiasm to find somewhere to camp, but the Gods decided to come down upon me again. I saw a European face for the first time in many days, they were also surprised by the encounter of another foreigner and came to introduce themselves, a lovely couple of whom the guy new this place very well, as he had been working here on some aid program a few years ago, now he was returning to visit friends here, he quickly offered to book me into his friends guest house, as he seemed to be close friends with everyone here, they all knew him and it was a joy to see their faces light up when they became reunited with him, obviously he had a great experience here. He told me what an incredible time he had, getting to live with and to know these people. I can quite imagine, he spoke fluent Nepalese and obviously got a great deal out of the experience. I thanked him for his help and had a great night, I was provided with a much needed hot shower and good food.

I was told to meet back at the bus at 5.00am to continue the rest of the journey, so with that I had set my alarm and settled down to sleep. I slept like the dead that night, to awake before my alarm went off, feeling completely refreshed and wide awake. I looked at the watch it read 5.00am and turned off the alarm, quickly got my things together and without any thought tried to get out. I forgot to tell them I wanted to be away early, there was no sign of life, and it was pitch black. I switched my headlamp on and traced my way out to the door that was locked, shit. I walked around making as much noise as I could hoping someone would get up, but nothing, no one. I tried the rear door to find another way out. No, I don't believe it I am locked in. I go up some stairs and find myself out onto a balcony. I look around and then I heard a voice in my mind saying

"You are thinking to leg it over there aren't you!"

Hmmmm maybe, I think to myself as I peer over the side, it looks not too far, but its dark and my fading batteries cast a yellow area of light which I cannot work out how far it is. I move a few pot plants and like a cat burglar I step out on to side. My bag is heavy and I calculate that I am going to drop like a sack of spuds, thud . . . . I drop drown maybe 3 meters, nothing breaks. I get up from underneath my rucksack, which had a nice soft landing thanks to turning in mid air and landing on top of me, therefore slightly winded I get up and brush myself off and walk quickly to where the bus was parked. I start to look around but it's completely deserted, this is funny I think, normally by this time things are starting to come to life. In Asia everyone gets up very early. I get to where the bus is parked, but the same thing there is no one. I think to myself that we should be going soon, then that feeling of doubt starts to saturate my mind, now a small alarm bell was saying alert! alert! Warning. OK what's gone wrong? What's happening? I look inside the bus and I can see the driver, he is asleep on the floor. I try to wake him but no matter how hard I try he does not move.

Maybe I was not as awake as I thought I was when I got up this morning. I started clawing around inside my mind trying to find an answer to this little mystery, and ah haaaa as usual there was no great mystery . . . . I check the time again it says 5.00am . . . . eh! . . . . Still . . . .! Hang on . . . . Suddenly I realise that time was not frozen at exactly 5.00am. I must have woken up to look at the alarm time that I had set, thinking this was the current time, I immediately swap it over from the alarm display to the current time, I looked, no way it was only 11.35pm . . . . bloody hell . . . . I had slept deep from 9pm and woke two and half hours later thinking it was time to go. All the pieces suddenly fell in to place clak, clak, clak . . . . Aaaaaah. Well ok there was no way I was going to lose face and go back to the guest house. I looked at the alternatives and climbed up on to the roof of the bus, then looked up at the incredibly clear, beautiful sky. The Milky Way stretched from horizon to horizon. I was instantly hypnotized in the dead of the night, complete solitude and stared deep into the dream time of that cosmos for a moment, just enough time to lose myself within all these stars, all these possibilities and thought to myself . . . .

"Yes I want to be here tonight."

I unpacked my sleeping bag and found a comfortable place to lay down and stared dreamily into the heavens. I started to chuckle to myself, which broke out into a full belly laugh from the bottom of my soul. I saw myself, an image within this universe, a point, a tiny dot upon this scene, this situation, this place, those words in my mind again . . .

"Yes . . . . I did not think this was going to happen today." again that statement seemed to echo throughout my life and continues to smack me in the back of my mind when I am least expecting it . . . . this time it said . . . .

"You stupid idiot."

The stupid idiot in me then stood up from the crowd he was hiding amongst to put up his hands, took a bow and said . . . .

"Yeah fair enough, that was a pretty good gaff though wasn't it."

I lay there and thought about all these things that I had experienced whilst travelling; the pleasures, the pains, the highs and the lows, and saw that they were the pieces to the puzzle I had been looking for; somewhere in between them I found balance, when all became calm, there was clarity, peace and acceptance, no one and nothing to fight any more, except my own clinging to the past and now I truly felt real freedom. I also discovered that mine is not the only culture in the world, no better, no worse just different bits of better and worse, but the differences, the journey and these discoveries make me humble. I hold dear in my heart all these experiences, and especially the people I have met and the exchange of time between us for the rest of my days. Thank you sincerely from my soul to yours. I and I together in this wonderful never ending Uni-verse.

12:21 am

Relaxed and calm I am
tumbling through the void I am infinitely small
as I am infinitely big with no beginning and no end
I am the detail upon detail ever expanding In every way
All is connected
the time the place
I am in no place
tried to grasp got to be quick this
greed obstructs me
my mind is trying
to win becoming
conscious within
this coma I am
almost there but
paused to think
tried to observe it
got to be quick
in this no-time place
just accept too late
it left as soon as it came
heard it whisper 'No not yet'
And faded into the past
I am Anita

Photographs and Artwork

Life is a mirror, draw or take a picture and show
me myself; all the highs and lows of the road
reveal your true faces, your true identity.

I found through travelling that there seems to be three
distinct characteristics to the human consciousness.

Three distinct phases that the mind reaches.

Three distinct levels of awareness.

Three personalities.

The magic

3

1.Unsure   2. Hopeful   3. Ecstatic.

China and huge mountains of the Himalayas behind.

Trekking near Dequin, timeless valleys.

Above, more endless valleys and raging rivers of
Chormas valley.

Below the treacherous trails that we had to navigate
at night with bags of shopping for Christmas day.

The heart warming smile of Chorma, below:
traditional kitchen, weaving magic with spices.

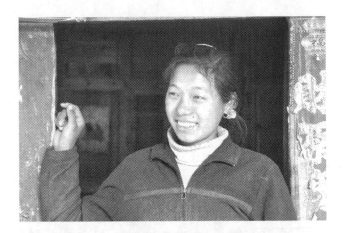

Haba Snow Mountain and tired legs, below:
the last steep icy push to the top.

Amazing cloud sea.
Below: Reaching the summit, a very cold and tired
me to the right, and my guide to the left just after
finishing smoking 20 Capstan full strength!!!

I will never complain again how heavy my baggage is, or how old I feel, or how long the road is.

Below: smoking seems to help them.

Above: tradition Tibet wedding costume.
Below: Chinese interior.

Nepalese family.

Below: never seen a foreigner, and dreaded formalities.

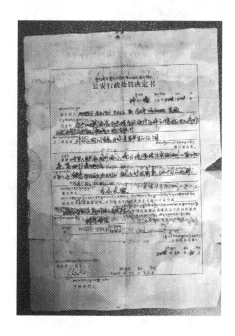

'Pala'
Shanfi, Shanfi. Galinos

Whatever miracle that you want to believe created us, God or a single celled organism that miraculously appeared out of the ether, then developed a consciousness and decided to start dividing, then decided to form complex structures, us! . . . . the fact is that we are that miracle, we all came from something, that single cell, or that infinite singularity and that moment in creation, whatever it was, we cannot be anything else other than that; we are the leaf on the tree, connected to the branch, the trunk, the seed . . . . we are all connected, even to God, we have that blueprint within us, consciousness existed first, then came material life, (the chicken or the egg?) we are and always have been that consciousness eternal and infinite, we just cannot remember whilst we are inhibited within the restrictions and distractions of this body, but we left clues here for ourselves, road signs, so that whilst we are driving through life in this vehicle we would notice them and take heed, so that hopefully we will be able to avoid all the obstacles and make it to paradise.